SMALL. FAMILY. BUSINESSES.

Special features of small family businesses and the consequences for company innovation processes

 The publications in the framework of the series WORK IN TRANSITION were created in the course of the transnational project **Job Transfer Europe** promoted by the Land North Rhine-Westphalia and the European Union (Community Initiative ADAPT).
Herstellung: Books on Demand GmbH
ISBN 3-8311-1278-9

Contents

1	**INTRODUCTION**	5
	The economic and social importance of small family businesses	5
	Social and economic developments	8
	Special features of small family businesses	12
2	**OBJECTIVES AND METHODS**	14
2.1	**Identification of interests and objectives**	14
2.2	**Methods**	15
2.3	**Profiles of the businesses under investigation**	18
3	**RESULTS**	34
3.1	**Small family businesses and the**	

	demands of modern economy	34
3.1.1	**Keyword globalisation**	35
	Focus globalisation	39
3.1.2	**Keyword marketing**	40
3.1.2.1	**Market observation**	40
	Focus market observation	46
3.1.2.1	**Knowledge of competitors**	47
	Focus knowledge of competitors	51
3.1.2.2	**Knowledge of customers**	52
	Focus knowledge of customers	56
	How do customer wishes change?	58
	Focus customers wishes	60
	Ecological material and production methods	61
	Focus ecology	64
3.1.2.3	**Customer contacts**	65
	Focus customer contacts	68
3.1.2.4	**Advertising**	69
	Focus advertising	77
3.1.3	**Keyword technology**	78
	Focus technology	84
3.1.4	**Keyword controlling**	86
	Focus controlling	90
3.1.5	**Keyword Employees and management style**	92
	Focus Employees	99

	Focus management style	109
3.2	**Special features of small family businesses**	111
3.2.1	**Relationship family – business**	111
3.2.2	**Objectives of small family businesses**	124
3.2.3	**Employees of small family businesses**	129
	Focus Employees	141
3.2.4	**Résumé: special features, advantages and disadvantages of small family businesses**	142
4	**RÉSUMÉ AND OUTLOOK**	147
4.1	**Special features of small family businesses**	148
4.2	**Globalisation as a challenge**	154
4.2.1	**Support of small family businesses- but how?**	158
	Investigation into the practice	160
	Consequences for consulting and support	161
5	**LITERATURE**	167

1 INTRODUCTION

THE ECONOMIC AND SOCIAL IMPORTANCE OF SMALL FAMILY BUSINESSES

- SOME FIGURES FROM GERMANY AND EUROPE

"In Germany there are more than 3.1 million small and medium-sized businesses. 99.6% of all businesses belong to the category of small and medium-sized businesses according to the latest statistic of turnover tax. These make 45.9% of all taxable turnover. They employ approximately 2/3 of all employees and train 4/5 of all apprentices. They contribute 52.1% of the gross value added of all businesses and effect 44.4% of all gross investments in Germany.

Beside their social importance small and medium-sized businesses above all have a huge economic importance as employers, training institutions, providers and innovators. They are so to speak the backbone of the German economy."[1]

---

[1] Bundesministerium für Wirtschaft, Arbeitsheft, Kleine und mittlere Unternehmen, Früherkennung von Chancen und Risiken, 1998, p.2

According to the report "Unternehmen in Europa - Fünfter Bericht - Daten 1994-1995", [2] the European Union counted "a total of 16,6 million private businesses, not counting agricultural undertakings in 1995. 99.9% of those had less than 500 employees and counted as "small and medium-sized enterprises", so-called SME. 14.7% million of these SMEs were "micro-enterprises" with less than ten employees. 7 million of those even without any employees at all. All in all 73% of all employees in the EU work in SMEs. The micro-enterprises with less than ten employees alone have a share of 32% of total employment. Germany is at the lower part of the scale with 23.5% of all employed people."[3]

That means that micro-enterprises with less than 10 employees provide nearly one quarter of all work places in Germany and therefore make an essential contribution to the labour market. Based on the latest total evaluation of all work places and employees in Germany of 1987, more than one third of all work places fall to small businesses with less than twenty employees.[4]

Small businesses with up to 20 employees, especially small family businesses are, however, only insufficiently included in the official statistics.[5] Therefore only very few reliable quantitative statements

---

[2] Unternehmen in Europa – Fünfter Bericht – Daten 1994-1995, ed.: Amt für amtliche Veröffentlichungen der Europäischen Gemeinschaften, Luxemburg, 1995
[3] cp Nationale Unterstützungsstelle ADAPT der Bundesanstalt für Arbeit, ADAPT-News No. 24, December 1999, p.1
[4] René Leicht, Der Beschäftigungsbeitrag kleinerer Betriebe in längerfristiger Sicht, in: R. Ridinger (ed.), Gesamtwirtschaftliche Funktionen des Mittelstandes, Berlin, 1997, p. 46

[5] „General statements on businesses are often based on official statistics. The official obligation to report provides ample basis for many problems.

can be made about them; also not on the proportion of family businesses.

According to Ballarini and Keese who performed an exemplary research project on the structures in small family businesses in 1991, we can assume that small companies with up to 20 employees are to a large extent family businesses.

This makes the small family businesses a very essential economic factor, many work places depend on them – and yet this type of business is comparatively unknown.

Small businesses with less than 20 employees are probably not included by these statistics, as there is no obligation to report for them. But those are the businesses that form the majority of the existing companies, especially family companies." K. Ballarini, D. Keese, Strukturen in kleinen Familienunternehmen, Veröffentlichungen des Instituts für Mittelstandsforschung, Universität Mannheim, ifm-Infodienst No. 1, p. 1

SOCIAL AND ECONOMIC DEVELOPMENT FOR SMALL FAMILY BUSINESSES

The speed of the changes of the economic framework conditions makes new and additional demands on the companies' adaptability and ability to learn. This basically also applies to the SFBes. Subject of this study is what aspects are possibly different here or have other consequences than for medium-sized or large businesses or non-family small businesses.

In the following we give a short outline of the aspects of economic changes, that we have looked into in detail:

- **Globalisation – internationalisation of the markets**

There is a noticeable acceleration of the internationalisation of economic relationships nowadays. This entails the necessity for an expansion of the observation and action horizon of the businesses. This affects, for instance, the gathering of information or transfer of information, marketing strategies, opening up of new markets and networking strategies.

- **Marketing**

The "buyer-market" with an still-growing competitive pressure forces businesses to strategic marketing measures, if they intend to survive on the market. Essential aspects of the development of marketing strategies are:

- *market observation*
- *knowledge of competition*
- *knowledge of customers*
- *advertising*

- Market observation

The basis of a well-planned marketing is the systematic observation and analysis of the market in order to recognise trends and developments in good time and be able to react accordingly. A most extensive knowledge of the competition and the customers are an important part of market knowledge.

- Knowledge of competition

Detailed information about the competition help the company to locate its own market position and is, if necessary, the basis for developing strategies for changes.

- Knowledge of customers

The expectations of many customers are subjected to fast change with ever increasing demands. The early recognition of customer wishes and the ensuing demand is an essential prerequisite for lasting success.

- Advertising

Advertising is the central instrument for the marketing for sales promotion. The investments into advertising of the economy are rising continuously[6] - a consequence of the increasing competitive pressure - ; the new media play an ever more important role here.

- **Technological development**

Owing to the fast technological development products and production procedures are changing faster all the time. In constantly increasing rhythms machines have to be updated or substituted in businesses dependent on technical equipment. Additionally nearly all sectors are affected by the fact that the new information and telecommunication technologies (IT, Internet, ISDN, etc.) are becoming more and more important, often independent of whether they actually contribute to the improvement of the company performance or an increase in sales.

- **Company controlling**

Constant availability and efficient keeping of the books is a must for every company in order to be able to react directly and as effectively as possible to economic developments. An expert professional bookkeeping is an essential basis for an effective controlling and it is especially important for small family businesses insofar as they often only possess a small basis of capital stock.

---

[6] In 1996 German companies invested approximately 555 billion marks into advertising for their goods; in 1987 it was still 33 billion marks. Cp. Vgl. Thomas Docter, Sponsoring und Werbung, in: Deutscher Industrie- und Handelstag (ed.), Umgang mit Presse, Medien, Öffentlichkeitsarbeit, p. 56

- **Team work and management style**

Rigid division of labour and steep hierarchies are no longer considered suitable forms of organisation for complex tasks and problems in a modern business. Small companies usually have less difficulties developing team-oriented forms of co-operation because of their lesser size than large companies. The size of the business often forces to hand-in-hand work. As team work is unthinkable without strengthening of responsibility and flexibility of the individual, a management style is necessary to support this. From the personnel development point of view a co-operative or helpful management style is more suitable for this purpose than a patriarchal or an authoritarian one.

- **Motivation of the Employees**

The performance of a business depends among other factors decisively on the motivation of the management and the Employees. What is the use of the latest technological equipment, if it is only half-heartedly adopted, what's the good of chic-styled flyers, if the employees do not feel able to identify with them? In these cases it is necessary to create the highest possible identity of interests between company requirements and visions on the one hand and the possibilities of new perspectives of the individual on the other hand. Besides the issues of earnings and possibility for careers, it is also a question of participation, esteem, commonly shared values, etc.

- **Ecology**

Consumer decisions for buying are oriented increasingly towards environmental compatibility of the supplied products.

It can be an advantage on the market for small companies to open up to customer wishes and take into consideration ecological criteria for production and material.

It was the aim of the presented study to investigate tendencies for the importance of the already mentioned requirements in the framework of a future-oriented company organisation in small family businesses, how they are managed and whether the family features are beneficial or whether they are rather a hindrance in this respect.

SPECIAL FEATURES OF SMALL FAMILY BUSINESSES

The decisive characteristic of a family business is that two social systems, family and company, overlap and interact here.

In the family the behaviour often follows subconscious patterns based on feelings and relationships of the individual family members, whereas conscious, task-and objective-oriented actions are important in the company.

Whereas the view is directed inwards in the family and relates to people and their relationships, the view of the company must be directed outwards, towards the market, the competition, and the potential customers.

The family is directed towards tradition and continuity, but the company has to react additionally to constant changes and innovations.

Whereas the individual belongs to the family by birth and is guaranteed closeness and care, the employees in a company are bound to the company by a contract and the co-operation is determined by their qualifications and their competencies.

The character of the relationships in a family are determined by affection, love, and trust. Relationships in the company are primarily determined by the functioning of the employees in the working process, where trust probably plays a part, too, but controlling is necessarily a part.

The communication structures in the family can be seen as spontaneous, emotional, well-tried out, and matter-of-fact, in contrast to the company, where you have to have well-reflected, structured, clear, and informative communication structures.

The interactions in the family have "natural" preconditions like parent-child relationships and division of labour according to the roles between man and woman. In the company the management, personnel guiding, and decision structures should be in the hands of competent professional people.

This understanding of the social system family and company serves as a foundation for our observation of the special features of small family businesses.

We presume chances as well as risks for necessary innovation processes in small family businesses through the interactions of the various structural elements.

2 OBJECTIVES AND METHODS

2.1 IDENTIFICATION OF INTERESTS AND AIMS

The investigation is to show

- how small family businesses react to the **demands** of a changing society and economy and
- what **consequences** can be deduced for company innovation processes
- what the **special features** of small family businesses are and
- what **advantages and disadvantages** result from this for the companies.

This is a field study, which is to provide first insights into an up to now more or less unprocessed field. Examples from the practice are to provide clues for possible special features and trends of small family businesses as well as possibly feature specific chances and risks. The objective is the collecting of information on this type of business which can, for instance, help consultants develop strategies closely adapted to their situation in co-operation with the small family businesses. The companies themselves can also benefit from knowing their special features more precisely and use this knowledge.

2.2 METHODS OF THE INVESTIGATION

The investigation was carried out exemplary on the basis of eight companies from different sectors. Common features of these small family businesses are, that at least 2 members of a family work in the company and the size of the company of no more than 20 employees.

Following instruments and methods were applied for the realisation of the investigation:

- checklist for the establishing of facts and data of the companies
- qualitative interviews with:
    - the owners of the companies
    - the family of the company owner
    - several employees
- minutes of the interview situation
- securing of the written material of the company
- inspection of the companies and minutes of the visits

The interviews were carried out with the help of an open interview guideline to give the interviewed people an optimal scope for their answers and to achieve open talks with the managers and the employees. All recorded talks were taken down in writing and then evaluated afterwards.

Period of the investigation

The interviews with the managers and employees of the participating small family businesses were carried out from October to December 1999.

Course and special features of the investigation

Contacting the small family businesses turned out to be a difficult task. Several attempts to contact them through chambers and other federations failed at first. Using our own business contacts, private contacts as well as the help of various institutions and representatives of federations at last provided the intended number of small family businesses of various sectors prepared to co-operate in this investigation.

We contacted a total amount of fourteen small family businesses, the investigation was carried out with eight small family businesses. Some of the addressed managers did not think that they could spare two to three hours of their limited time for the investigation. One female owner talked very openly about her situation as a small family business in a first contact talk, but was not prepared to continue the interview with a recorder. Only one manager of a small family business said that he was not interested in such an investigation. All companies, even those that took part in our investigation, had extremely little time to spare. The interview times were adapted to the time the managers had, which meant for instance that one interview was carried out on a Sunday afternoon, another interview late at night during the week and a further one was only possible at 7.00 a.m.

The interviews with the owner families took an average of 1½ to 2 hours and took place in their homes in half the cases and in the companies in the other half. In most cases the interviews were held with both or several of the family members working in the company. In two cases, where this was not possible, the wife had family obligations.

The interviews with the employees took approximately half an hour. Three interviews with employees took place on the premises of the company and in two cases they were held during working hours. The other two interviews took place after working hours. Unfortunately it was not possible to interview employees in every company owing to problems with making an appointment.

The interviews were mostly held in a relaxed, concentrated atmosphere. Small breaks resulted from having to care for children, answering the telephone, or from the fact that the business was continuing and the customers had to be served.

It is worth mentioning that the limited time resources of the small family businesses were not felt in the interviews. All involved interviewed people took time to answer all the questions and showed an interest in the investigation beyond the interview.

2.3 PROFILES OF THE BUSINESSES UNDER INVESTIGATION

- **Conrad & Conrad - Messe und Ausstellungsservice** [Fair and Exhibition Service - the translator] - **coMa**

A. *The start of the company*

The company has existed since 1985. The owners are brothers, with one of them the managing director. Another three members of the family work in the company. The company became a GmbH [Gesellschaft mit beschränkter Haftung = limited liability company – the translator] in 1999.

B. *Products - Services*

Coma operates a service for fairs and exhibitions and offers all sorts of services linked with that. Stalls are developed and planned together with the customers and built according to the customer wishes and put up in the respective fair locations.

C. *Location of the company*

The company is situated in a small industrial settlement at the edge of Rheinberg, the Rheinberg industrial park.

D. *Opening hours / availability*

According to statements by the interviewed managers it is open from 9.00 a.m. to 6 p.m.

There is someone available all the time and afterwards customer queries are recorded by an answering machine or a fax machine and taken care of as soon as possible.

E. Premises

The company consists of a large shop with more than 1.000 sqm store space and large garage area with machine equipment as well as neighbouring office space on the first floor, which is very spacious. Employees facilities are located in the basement of the building. An ingenious storing system developed over 15 years as well as a loading ramp for lorries, which is roofed and closed in, so that the lorries can be put away safely at night, are integrated in these new premises.

F. Employees

Five members of the family work for the company, beyond that there are five employees as well as some part-time Employees and trainees depending on season and demand. There is also a cleaning person on a half-time job.

- **Elektro Goß GmbH – Fach- und Lichttechnik**
  [electrical lighting specialists]

A.   The start of the company

The company in its present form has existed since the summer of 1990. Herr Goß was employed in a large company as an electrician, but had to leave this company because it went bankrupt. The company has the legal form of an GmbH [Gesellschaft mit beschränkter Haftung = limited liability company – the translator]. Herr Goß started up the company with three childhood friends.

B.   Products - Services

The Elektro Goß GmbH has specialised in lighting systems as well as electrical engineering of all types especially in the field of shop fittings. Among their tasks is the planning and co-ordination of architecture and lighting in shop installations. These services are offered to a variety of buyers, from restaurants to high-class boutiques. Elektro Goß is also involved in the field of planning and building of large electrical plants as well as special lighting systems, supply of parts, and Europe-wide construction jobs. The provision of other, non-electrical work in the shop installation is being executed on more and more and is seen as a customer service by Elektro Goß.

C.   Location of the company

The company is situated in a very rural area, in Welver-Borgeln, approximately six kilometres from Soest. The nearest motorway is about 8 km. The company resides in a new building, which serves as company seat, workshop, storeroom, and office, but could be converted into two or three flats any time. The building had just been completed at the time of the interview.

D.   Opening hours / availability

According to Herr Goß himself he is available in his company from early in the morning to late at night. Customers and his colleagues can also get hold of him on his mobile all day.

E.   Company premises

The company premises are brand new and consist of a large storehouse on the ground floor, which also serves as a workshop. As the fitters work mainly away from the company, the work places do not take up much room. The storehouse serves on the one hand as storeroom for material, which will be fitted at the customer's later, on the other hand it is a store for spare parts for those services, which the company provides in the way of repairs and general maintenance and services. The offices and a meeting room are on the first floor. They are well lit and furnished pleasantly. Large windows let in plenty of light and allow a generous view into the countryside. The location and direction to the light of the building were selected on purpose to be able to convert the company building into a house for a family later.

F.   Employees

The company employs eight people. All are full-time Employees and are paid in excess of the agreed scale. The boss has known three of his co-workers closely for a long time. His wife works in the company part-time in the bookkeeping, office organisation, on the telephones and the correspondence, when her husband is away on business or the work load demands it.

- **The Götterspeise company – party service, catering, health food, snacks**

A. *The start of the company*

The business in its present form has existed since May 1998. Before the start of the company they cooked health food for the kindergarten that the company owners' children go to. Then the kitchen at home became too small for all the cooking and at first just a place for the cooking was looked for. The favourable terms for the rent led to the taking up of a shop and so through the cooking for the Kindergarten a catering and buffet service and the sale of health food and eventually the Götterspeise company in its present form developed, which now offers lunches and differs from the classical health food shops by its manifold goods. The company name [Götterspeise = jelly – the translator] was chosen on purpose to avoid associations with a pure health food shop in contrast to names like e.g. Kornkammer [granary – the translator], Naturwurzel [nature root], etc.

B. *Products - services*

The services of the Götterspeise company comprise 4 fields:

1. organic snacks and lunches (all weekdays, cake on Sundays)
2. delivery of lunches to companies and kindergartens
3. buffets and catering service for private people, groups, clubs, etc.
4. sale of health foods in companies.

The service of Götterspeise comprises the consulting of customers, the satisfaction of special wishes, and the delivery of the goods to the customer.

C. Location of the company

At the beginning it was considered wise not to open up a shop in Essen-Steele but to go to Essen-Rüttenscheid, where customers were presumed who could identify more with a health snack bar. Because of the favourable offer of a shop in Essen-Steele and the fact that the owner family also live in Essen-Steele. the business is in the middle of the district of Essen-Steele. The shop is situated next to a street with a lot of traffic with very little parking places, opposite an arts centre, with a large shop front which allows a good look in. A butcher's shop was in those premises for 38 years previously.

D. Opening hours / availability

The opening hours are from Monday to Friday from 8.00a.m. to 8.00 p.m., Saturdays from 9.00 a.m. to 2.00 p.m., and Sundays from 3.00 p.m. to 5.00 p.m. Outside these opening hours the Götterspeise company can be contacted via a fax machine in the shop.

E. The company premises

The total size of the premises is around 70 square metres. A large shop window with the firm's logo and the current offers invites you to take a look into the shop. The sales room, which also serves as the snack bar, is approximately 18 square metres and it is equipped with several seats for customers. Varying small exhibitions of photos or paintings invite you to look and stay. Additionally there is a 20 sqm kitchen, a storeroom of 12 sqm, a small work place for the office work of the company, a cellar of 10 sqm, which is also used for storage, as well as 8 sqm free space, toilet and hall.

F. Employees

Apart from the owner couple there are two employees in the company who take turns to do the shifts during the week. Both work on a 630,- DM basis.

- **Killat GmbH – builders and tiles**

A. The start of the company

The tiling company Killat has existed for 16 years. Both husband and wife come from self-employed families. The Killat company is a GmbH [see above].

B. Products – services

The Killat company works in the fields tiling, bricklaying, and (if necessary) plumbing. This applies to indoor and outdoor work. As a rule they tile baths. As an additional service the Killat company takes over the realisation of orders beyond their part of the job. When jobs are necessary, that go beyond the usual scope of the company, they are either carried out by the company themselves or other companies are commissioned.

C. Location of the company

The company is situated in the north of Essen in the district of Altenessen. The building with flats is on grounds with a yard, and comprises storeroom, workshop, and parking places for the Killat company. It is the property of the family.

D. Opening hours

Work begins at 7.00 a.m., from this time onwards the company is available. The "normal" working hours end around 4 p.m. The company is, however, available for customers on the telephone until 10 p.m.

E. Premises of the company

There is a workshop, a yard, and a small room for shelter. The employees meet in the yard of the Killat company in the morning before work and go to the building sites together in the company vehicles. As the Killat company does not sell tiles or stores them for their customers, no large storerooms are necessary.

F. Employees

Apart from the owner couple there are three more employees in the company, one of them the Frau Killat's nephew and so part of the family. There are no apprentices, but a number of trainees working for the Killat company for a few months or weeks.

- **Mayer & Heck GmbH – books and media – representation of publishing houses**

A. The start of the company

The married couple Mayer and Heck has two companies, both in the legal form of a GmbH. The one company, Leseband GmbH, has the task to sell books in the design centre Essen and to help organise exhibitions and fairs. This company has existed since 1995 with Frau Heck being the managing director.

The second company, which has the bigger turnover, is the Meyer & Heck GmbH. This company represents about 10 publishing houses in NRW. The company has existed since 1991 with the shareholders Ewald Mayer and Ulrike Heck.. Ewald Mayer was in the publishing house business before this.

B. Products - services

The shop in the design centre sells books, which have to do with design in the widest sense, and provides an adequate range of literature for exhibitions. Furthermore small book fairs are also staged there. This serves to let the specialised publishing houses, that Mayer & Heck work for, exhibit their products. The main business lies with the representation of publishing houses by the Mayer & Heck GmbH.

The services of the Mayer & Heck GmbH consist of setting up a sales promotion co-operation by product schooling for certain segments offered to booksellers.

C. Location of the company

The company consists primarily of an office in the freehold flat of the couple in Essen-Steele. The Leseband GmbH company exists mainly as a shop in the design centre of the Zeche Zollverein in Essen Katernberg.

D. Opening hours

There are no official opening hours in this trade. The two publishing house representatives are, however, available all the time via email, fax, and answering machine. The opening hours of the shop in the design centre are not known to us.

E. Premises of the company

The office in the freehold flat is equipped with a large work table for shipments and two PC-working place, very state-of-the-art and professional.

F. Employees

Three students work for the Leseband GmbH, each four hours a day, on weekdays in the shop in the design centre. The work of the Mayer & Heck GmbH is largely done by the owner couple.

• Mörsheim, the allergy service

A. The start of the company

Herr Mörsheim registered his trade in 1989 as a self-employed person. He started with a cleaning service for floors and carpeting. In the course of the last 6 years a new business idea grew, which, together with his wife, he has been realising for more than a year now. This is a health service for allergic people at home and at work.

B. Products - services

The Mörsheim company sees itself as a health service in the field of services for the allergic.

Their services comprise the cleaning of all types of upholstery, bedding, and other furniture infested by household mites in order to create a living situation suitable for allergic people. Furthermore they sell anti-allergy products like bedding, blankets, upholstery covers, etc. The consulting proportion of the customer service is very large. Great emphasis is laid not on selling short-term, but on a long-term competent consulting for the purchase of quality products. By stocking a number of products direct shipment is possible. Products that are not on stock at the Mörsheim company are shipped via the production companies with the Mörsheim company taking over the shipping, so that they can guarantee that the ordered goods will be at the customer's address within three days Germany wide.

C.   Location of the company

The company is situated in a small place called Unterbruch near Heinsberg at the Dutch border, approximately 20-30 km from Roermond. The fact that the company has its seat there has to do with the wish of the family to live in a quiet and secluded place. The house of the family is also the seat of the company.

D.   Opening hours / availability

Like in so many family businesses the times when somebody is available are very generously proportioned. The owner couple did not mention any time limits, they are available per phone or fax all the time.

E.   Premises of the company

The office of the Mörsheim company is situated next to the kitchen in an annex. The garage of the house where the tools and materials are kept, can be counted as a further company room.

F. Employees

Apart from the couple and the father-in-law who helps where it is necessary, there is a part-time help, who has been with the company a long time.

- **The Prägo-Patrizen company** [Patrize = male mold - the translator]

A. The start of the company

The company has a long history, although not in its present form. It goes back to the twenties, when the grandfather of the present (female) owner started the business. The company produces material for relief-stamping techniques. The firm in its present form has existed since the seventies. The present owner took over the company in 1992 after studying sociology and has since then worked in the company with her mother.

B. Products - services

The Prägo-Patrizen company works in a market gap and the produced articles for relief stamping techniques are sold world-wide. The additional services relate largely to the overcoming of the hurdles on behalf of the customers existing world-wide by customs regulations.

C.   Location of the company

The company is situated in a residential area of Oberhausen in a building with four flats. The company premises take up the whole of the first floor, the cellar, and the yard.

D.   Opening hours / availability

The opening hours are from 9.00 to 18.00 hours. After hours the company can be contacted by answering machine and fax machine.

E.   Company premises

Two office rooms and an area for consultations with customers are situated at the front part of the building. At the back are the production rooms. There is a small separate room for the stamping and printing machine (Heidelberger Tiegel), a larger room serves as a storeroom and for the shipping. This is also the location of the production place for the chemical material, which the company produces. Additionally there is the cellar, also used as a storeroom.

F.   Employees

The Präge-Patrizen company employs solely women. This was not originally planned, it just happened.

Apart from mother and daughter there are two more full-time employees with differing working hours, both working less than 38.5 hours, and a temporary help also with flexible working hours, also working less than 38.5 hours.

SMALL. FAMILY. BUSINESSES.

- ## The builders Berthold Rauen

A.   *The start of the company*

The firm has existed since May 14th 1992. Both husband and wife come from self-employed families.

B.   *Products - services*

The company works mainly in interior building with a wide range of jobs. The emphasis lies on dry building. The customer is also offered complete solutions in the way of building authorities and total organisation of all restructuring works for the building, the flat, or company and office rooms.

C.   *Location of the company*

The seat of the company is in an almost purely residential area; apart from a shop and services centre opposite them.

D.   *Opening hours / availability*

The company is available from seven in the morning to late at night via the telephone of the family, again it is not seldom as late as 10 p.m. that the wife answers the telephone to answer customers' requests.

Work starts at 7.00 a.m. and ends at different times depending on the current job.

E. Company premises

The workshop, storeroom, an office, which is at present not used, and the parking places for the company cars are in the yard behind the family flat, which is in a block of flats.

F. Employees

Apart from the owner couple four full-time employees work for the company.

3 RESULTS

3.1 SMALL FAMILY BUSINESSES AND THE DEMANDS OF MODERN ECONOMY

Globalisation and economic change put new demands on businesses. Companies that want to secure their survival on a long-term basis have to meet those demands. - Does this trend apply to small businesses, particularly to small family businesses? At which points does it explicitly have an effect on them? And how do small family businesses meet these new demands? We have investigated the attitudes, experiences and future plans of the companies of the study on following points:

- *Globalisation (internationalisation of markets)*
- *Marketing*
- *Communication techniques*
- *Economic controlling*
- *Employees, management style, and communication*

3.1.1 Keyword globalisation

Internationalisation of markets

Europe is an important topic for the small family businesses - half of the companies interviewed by us have some sort of contact in the European region.

The market Europe

The Elektro Goß GmbH, for instance, has a customer in Spain, who has decided to have its electrical fittings for a restaurant done by a German firm after the German safety norms (VDE-regulations [- Verband Deutscher Elektrotechniker - the federation of electrical engineers - the translator]), which have to be adopted because of the adaptation in the EU. The Goß company has seized this chance and therefore inevitably possesses a broader knowledge of the European market. Even though the proportion of the European customers at present "only" comes to about 5% of the total turnover of the company, the possibility for an expansion is seen here. The European market therefore plays a role for the future of the Goß company.

> *"We definitely want to seize that chance, because that is the market, where you can make money. There is no more to be gained with the work around the corner from here."*
> (Herr Goß, Elektro Goß GmbH)

The coMa company has been working in the European area for a while and is at present thinking about a co-operation partner in

Italy. They do mention, however, that working in other countries is not easy for German fair- and exhibition workers. The logistics and the infra-structural preconditions of fairs/exhibitions in Germany are described as definitely better and more advantageous than abroad.

Customers from abroad play a decisive role for the Prägo-Patrizen company.

> "Two thirds of our customers are abroad, world and Europe-wide, and one third is in Germany."
> (Sabine Grossarth jun., Prägo-Patrizen)

Information source Europe

The Mörsheim company has a large interest in getting to know more about the discussions on allergies from our north-European neighbours.

> "For our customer wishes we first turned to the Netherlands, who are much further in this field as well as Sweden and Denmark."
> (Herr Mörsheim, the Mörsheim-Allergieservice company)

According to Herr Mörsheim the Dutch are "leading in Europe" in questions of fighting against allergies and the development in this field is watch closely by the Mörsheim company.

> *"The Netherlands, for instance have the "Milbenpäpstin" [house-mites - pope - the translator], who has set things in motion."*
> (Herr Mörsheim, the Mörsheim-Allergieservice company)

The European market and the development of the sector in Germany in general does have an effect on the publishing house agency Mayer & Heck, even though they do not regard themselves as acutely affected by the developments on the European book market.

> *"If the book price maintenance is going to continue, we will still have a clientele large enough to warrantee the overall provision with books even in rural areas. As soon as the price maintenance is abolished we have the problem - like in France or in England, that a massive dying of book seller shops will set in, because the customers will buy their stuff in the large chain stores. We will not be so strongly affected, as we are oriented strongly on specialised books, and they are not affected by that. The larger will then start playing a bigger role."*
> (Ewald Mayer, the Mayer & Heck GmbH)

The technical innovations in the building trade are of interest to the building company Rauen and they are observed, like a general price development, beyond the German borders. You cannot, however, call this a systematic comparison.

"Does it play a role for you to have an international comparison of what other companies and building trades do?"

> "We are always interested in new techniques, other equipment. The interest in the prices is natural, but not so that it would have a direct effect."
> (Herr Rauen, Baugeschäft Rauen)

The Kilat GmbH has not yet given a thought to the international development of the tiling market.

The Götterspeise company presumes that there are very few health food shops in combination with ecological snack bars either in Germany or internationally, and the international market plays a minor role.

Europe is far away

Along with the family businesses with more or less interest in internationalisation of markets and information we met with an equal amount of companies with no activities at all in this direction. The reason for this lies with those companies being basically satisfied with their present business situation and that they see their target group rather locally. From their viewpoint there is no necessity to invest time and money into the widening of their radius.

Focus globalisation

Summarising the statements of the interviewed companies it seems that the differing approaches of the small family businesses to the topic globalisation have various reasons:

- it depends on the sector

- it depends on the economic pressure to gain new clientele

- it certainly also depends on the respective personality (previous knowledge, interest, no prejudices against new media, etc.)

- and sometimes it is just a question of pure chance: for instance when the activity is a reaction to an actual customer's request.

3.1.1 Keyword marketing

Growing competition and increasing customers' expectations make it increasingly necessary to hold one's own market position by methodical market strategies. - So much to the general trend.

Small businesses in particular presumably have to deal with increased competition e.g. by new businesses or illicit labour. How do they defend their market position? We interviewed the companies on four focal points of marketing:

- *Market observation*
- *Knowledge of competitors*
- *Knowledge of customers*
- *Advertising*

3.1.1.1 Market observation

All interviewed small family businesses stated, that they know "their market" and have a good idea of the developments of the market. We noticed differences in the way as well as in the intensity of the market observation. Some companies have a more intuitive approach to the demands of the market, others tackle the changes more specifically and take specific measures to survive on the market.

....from intuitive to organised

> "What do you know about your market? Where is the development going?

> "My planning does not depend on what I read in specialised journals. I tend to rely on my intuition."
> (Frau Grossarth jun., Prägo-Patrizen)

> „The ecological markets still have development potential and they are said to possess growth potential."
> (Frau Hofen, Götterspeise)

This assessment is based on reports and articles of the federation news of the natural foods shops, which the Götterspeise company subscribes to and uses as information source on the current market developments.

> "There seem to be two types of development. On the one hand the demand for our labour seems to be increasing, on the other hand there is a price decline. We are relatively lucky, because we are flexible and can jump at request, our company is not too small and not too big, but we are following the direction of the development with suspense. This is all experience from my own practice or knowledge gained from specialised journals."
> (Herr Rauen, Baugeschäft Rauen)

Frau Killat also states clearly, that practical experience with the customers give her insight into how the market is developing. Regulars and "safe major accounts" contribute to the fact, that the company on the whole is doing well. And "lulls" in the sector are explained with seasonal fluctuations.

> "Because we have so many old customers, including estate agents and building societies with their many houses, where there is always some work to do, we have a lot of work coming to us. There is a lull in every building company. In winter there is no work to do outdoors, that is all done."
> (Frau Killat, Killat GmbH)

Hrr Goß emphasizes, that the development is leading ever faster to the new technologies. As manager of the Elektro Goß GmbH he shows a positive attitude to this development and he has realised that here lies the future market for the company. He informs himself about the new developments in the specialised fairs, forums and specialised journals.

> "…..we get our information at fairs; the industrial fairs in Hanover, Frankfurt, and Dortmund. I visit them myself in order to get information on the latest techniques. …There are new techniques, which will come, and we see that positively. Other companies don't do that. I have no idea whether they are not in the position to do so or if they don't want to."
> (Herr Goß, Elektro Goß GmbH)

Herr Goß observes the development of the future IT transfer very attentively and he is getting ready for the coming new technology to be among the first to be able to handle these techniques. His contacts to companies working in the field of information and telecommunication technology (IT) contribute to that.

> "We intercept new developments like daylight technique, Internet, and new techniques which will affect the electricians, and will commercialise them. An example: the possibilities for data transmission by normal copper cable are exhausted, the machines are, however, much further developed. There is a new project with light wave conductor cables, where the question is, can we do that or do we want to do that. That means an investment of one hundred thousand marks for tools and training. That is a real demand on us. It means going to a week's training to be able to work the new tools and you have to ask yourself whether you want to invest that. Some say, I haven't got the money and I don't want the stress of going back to school at the age of forty or fifty."
> (Herr Goß, Elektro Goß GmbH)

One of the objectives for the year 2000 is the participation of Elektro Goß in the Euroshop-exhibition at Düsseldorf, an exhibition for shop designers and equippers. with their own stall.

> "…our sector is changing at the moment insofar as a few years ago the discussion was running along the line "do we still need representatives for publishing houses because of electronic data transfer" and that has shown, how the profession of the representative of a publishing house is really changing at the moment. We look at it that way, that if the representative doesn't adapt to the changed market situation, then you are going to be the loser, then the publishing house is going to

> *manage without you.. the pressure on us representatives is great. On the one hand we need good publishers whose books are easy to sell, on the other hand we have to convince the booksellers and make them good offers for their benefit and ours. The second problem is the concentration on the market. The publishing houses are buying each other out and that means representative teams who used to have the small publishing houses are shrinking, there is a considerable amount of change at the moment."*
> (Frau Heck, Mayer & Heck GmbH)

The concentration of publishing houses and new technical possibilities endanger the subsistence of the "classical" representative. The Mayer & Heck company has realised this and understood it as an incentive to adapt to the new market. The development of the sector is observed closely.

> *"There are about two hundred companies involved in equipping fairs and exhibitions in Germany, organised in the umbrella organisation of the exhibition builders. Furthermore we get a part of our information from journals, that are sent to us. …the demands have increased. Twenty years ago a trestle table was put up – that was it. Then the people hung up pictures in the stalls, decorated the tables, and so this developed ever further. Events are planned with everything around, invitations, advertising outdoors, advertising on taxis to make*

> *the relatively expensive event as efficient as possible."*
> (Andreas Conrad, coma GmbH)

Andreas Conrad also mentions that the exhibition builders have to meet the increasing demands to the stalls on the customers' side and also come to terms with the ever decreasing finances on the clients' side and that the competitive pressure has risen considerably in the last few years.

> *"The field of allergies is still hardly talked about, but that is not going to continue that way. The need to save is not achievable for the health insurances without service companies. The affected people will need help more and more. When we are known we have a certain market. Thirty percent of the population and as a prophylaxis 100%. This has made us realise that new channels of distribution have to be created in the next few years. A specialist will be needed for the field of allergies in the future, the normal doctor, pharmacist, or shops for medical aids can't meet the requirements."*
> (Herr Mörsheim, Mörsheim-Allergy Service)

The Mörsheim company sees the present market for an allergy service in close context with the willingness of the health insurances to take over the costs. The health insurances show a tendency towards the topic of allergies and to invest more in the field of prophylaxis. Through the health insurances the Mörsheim allergy service has the possibility to present their products for allergy-free living and working as well as allergy-consulting to the affected households, companies, and individual people. Through the co-operation with health insurances, doctors, and shops for medical aids a large market is seen for the future. This was confirmed to Herr Mörsheim by a management consultant, whom he works with occasionally.

Focus market observation

We noticed, that in the companies questioned by us the degree of organisation from information gaining to market development stands in close correlation with the size of the company (turnover, number of employees)

Besides it seems to be a question of outward pressure (compare also keyword globalisation), how much energy is invested into the observation of developments.

A further factor is that the innovative company that is just establishing in a new developing market will observe this with much more attentiveness than e.g. the old crafts company in a traditional sector.

3.1.2.1 Knowledge of competitors

...the first impression
what I don't know I don't have to worry about!

> "...we worry very little about competition. Everybody looks after themselves. There is no power struggle.
> (Frau Killat, the Killat GmbH)

> "There are certain standard prices for services that are standard services – a square metre of tiles or a square metre of bricks; they have to conform to the morals, you mustn't exaggerate. Otherwise it's secondary – give or take competition – our services are very specific."
> (Herr Rauen, Baugeschäft Rauen)

Half of the companies stated that competition plays rather a minor role to no role at all. Nevertheless all companies are confronted with competition and take notice of it.

...the second impression
They are ruining us!

Illicit workers who are ruining the prices and ruining the reputation of the trade are a serious problem for the company.

> "I have to tell you quite honestly, that the many illicit workers from the former Eastern bloc are ruining the market. The customers are often very disappointed. They have to calculate with their money, it's always at least six thousand marks. Then the Polish workers come and they do the work for one thousand. They ruin the prices, because they have no idea of the business. The bathroom is then done haphazardly, doesn't look good and the customers have no addressee, have no one to complain to."
>
> (Frau Killat, the Killat GmbH)

What "the official" competitors can perform and have to offer becomes apparent when they have to measure themselves against them.

> "...I have two lines, two main lines. The one is a large proportion of private customers, and the other is the more professional part with an architect and other customers. You have to realise that both are important. The price structure is different. It applies more to the second line with the architect. There we are confronted with "Your competitors XY offer that for such and such", that happens.
>
> (Herr Rauen, Baugeschäft Rauen)

The Götterspeise company that sees itself more or less without competition in the field of ecological snack bars, used to look at the more distant natural foods shops and snack bars at least in the starting phase of the shop. They know the other natural foods shop in the town district and they emphasize, that they differ from this shop. That means, that they bear competition in mind, want to differ, and provide new and other services and products.

The Mörsheim company, which declares itself as having no competition of its kind, also thinks it important not to lose their competitors out of sight.

> "The way we do things (we are, - the author) without competition, in some areas, however (thare is, the author) competition. Every shop for medical aids is a competitor, especially those, that do not work quite up to the rules. Also pharmacies and all those, that want to sell products more or less without consulting the customer..."
> (Herr Mörsheim, Mörsheim, Allergy-service)

While one part does not really seem to be very aware of what role the observation of competition can play, or underestimates their knowledge of their competitors and does not attribute any greater importance to this field, the other half of the companies belong to the rather attentive observers.

...the third impression!
"I know quite a lot about our competitors!" (Herr Goß, Elektro Goß GmbH)

The comparison shows clearly, that the companies, who keep up to date with the market development also observe their competitors, their services, and products closely.

SMALL. FAMILY. BUSINESSES.

> "…I'm glad, that our competitors do not undertake the trips to say Berlin or Munich on Mondays at four o'clock like we do, to work there for a week."
> (Herr Goß, Elektro Goß GmbH)

> "We don't have a lot of competition, because we have specialised in a field, we have chosen lighting techniques. We have greater possibilities through the service, that we offer. …We can also offer a reasonable follow-up service, that means, the customer can purchase parts through us."
> (Herr Goß, Elektro Goß GmbH)

This small family business has managed the development towards a specialisation mainly by the observation of the competition, because they realised correctly that locally there wasn't a big enough market.

> ""We definitely want to seize that chance, because that is the market, where you can make money. There is no more to be gained with the work around the corner from here."
> (Herr Goß, Elektro Goß GmbH)

An improvement of their market chances was the step that Mayer & Heck took, when they created a co-operation out of a competitive situation by merging with another company of publishing house representatives, with more possibilities to react to the market, to offer a better service to the customers and to help each other.

> "the thing is, that we have been working together with another company of representatives for six months now, so that we have created a co-operation out of a competitive situation to be able to look after our customers even better. ... This is a novelty in this sector, nobody has done that up to now..."
>
> (Herr Mayer, Mayer & Heck GmbH)

Smaller co-operation activities can also be found in the crafts sector, especially where other firms have to be involved to complete a commission.

> "If we have too much to do, we give work away; for instance we do parqueting, but when there isn't enough time, we let others do it."
>
> (Herr Rauen, Baugeschäft Rauen)

Only the Prägo-Patrizen company shows up well on the market, primarily through its uniqueness. The company makes products for relief-molding techniques. The observation of competition plays a minor part. The work of the company takes place in a market gap. It would, however, not be possible to do business in Germany alone. Two thirds of their customers come from abroad.

Focus: Knowledge of competitors

Information on one's competitors are available at all companies, they do, however, differ in the

> degree of attentiveness towards competition. For some it is very important to observe their competitors, to process new developments and use them for the good of their own companies, others do not see this necessity, because they are in a market gap, think of themselves as unique or are satisfied with their own situation.
>
> For some companies the observation of the competition has had a positive effect and there were some practical consequences. In one case the occupation with their competition led to a co-operation with another company, in another the knowledge of their competition was decisive for the company concentrating on a specific market and a future-oriented business policy in the areas training and qualification with a view to future market areas.

3.1.2.3   Knowledge of customers

Where do the customers come from?
....from next door and everywhere

With the exception of the ecological snack bar and the natural foods shop, where the customers come mainly from the town district, the clientele of the interviewed companies is local as well as regional and also supra-regional. The small family businesses, that have a bigger turnover and are larger have an international clientele, so does the Prägo-Pratrizen company, who have had two thirds of their clientele abroad from the start owing to their special product. In the case of the other companies the clientele abroad results for one from the type of service they offer (fair/exhibition builders) and in the other case it was a deliberate expansion of the regular business (Elektr Goß GmbH). The Mörsheim company is thinking of a nation-wide as well as a north-west European expansion of their market. The Mayer & Heck company is limited to NRW owing to the company structure.

How does one recognise customer wishes? The personal conversation is the best way

> "The customers voice their wishes and we ask what they want. We once intended to do this in writing, but up to now we had no time for that. We haven't got a list of customers, but we have a file of the buffet customers and their buffet wishes."
> (Frau Hofen, the Götterspeise company)

> „The customers approach us, they want something from us. They ring, I make an appointment with them, and my husband goes to see them, looks at the job, takes everything down, and after fifteen years of experience he can tell the customers how much it is going to cost. Many customers want to know how much it will be, when we go to see them. Many make an estimate, I send it to them, we have to calculate first. Having worked fifteen years in my job, I know approximately how much it

will be. My husband has a look at the bathroom, our customers buy the tiles themselves, because that would be too much work for us. There are so many nice and reasonably priced tiles."
(Frau Killat, Killat GmbH)

„...you get to know customer wishes when talking to them., I go see our customers with a bottle of wine once every three months, or now at Xmas with a calendar, and then we talk about the past year and all the things that weren't so hot."
(Herr Goß, Elektro Goß GmbH)

The companies want the personal conversation with the customers. This applies the other way round to the customers. The personal conversation takes place every day. It can take place on the building site, in the company on the phone, when delivering ordered goods, personally at a fair, when installing electrical cables, or in a consultation, like in the case of the Mörsheim company, which knows a lot about their customers and their wishes and problems. When the boss isn't available for the customer during the day, the wishes and requests are taken down during the day or even into the night in the family living quarters by the wife, who works for the company, who then either deals with them herself or passes them on to her husband at night.

The direct contact to the customer to take down their wishes is mentioned as the most important item by the interviewed companies. In order to deal with the customer wishes more precisely all companies carry out consulting in all companies.

> "I would say most of this happens intuitively; or rather goes back to experience, and I have noticed that a most extensive consulting is as a rule the best way; for one to help the customer realise what he really wants, because that is usually very vague. There is often quite a muddle – we would like to, but we don't know how and what and where -,and if you take a bit of time for that, we usually get thanked for it."
>
> (Herr Rauen, Baugeschäft Rauen)

The Mörsheim company, which also gets to know a good part of the customer wishes in the consulting, has developed additional possibilities for gaining extra knowledge of their customers in the European countries.

> "We first turned to the Netherlands, who are so much more advanced in this field as well as Sweden and Denmark for our customer wishes. The German problem is, that we have to start rethinking. The Germans don't ask what they have to do for their health, but what their health insurance will pay for. We have fourteen million people, who are sensitive to household dust mites and five millions of those are already diseased, and from my experience around seventy-five percent children. We have to teach the people to provide a symptom-free life, and so help a child to stay with a normal allergy and not to get a step further to asthma. The number of allergic people is increasing all the time, no doctors can help there, no allergy service, we have a real big problem there. We

want to sell sensible things and most things that we sell need to be explained. There is also the big difficulty, that there are no standardised payments from the health insurances in the federal states of Germany."

(Herr Mörsheim, Mörsheim Allergy-Service)

In addition to the customer talks the coMa company employs further targeted methods to shape customer wishes more precisely and to put the expectations in concrete terms., for instance checklists to determine straight away what the customer possesses in the way of prerequisites and what is missing. These checklists serve to specify and realise customer wishes.

There is a special situation at the Prägo-Patritzen company. They do not neglect the personal contact with their customers, but owing to the fact that two thirds of their customers are from abroad, the fax machine is the central communication medium in the evening hours for requests and orders. Wishes for alterations or extension of the range of products relate primarily to services of the company for instance help with dealing with the customs formalities in various countries.

Focus knowledge of customers

The small family businesses under investigation use several ways to recognise customer wishes. The most important instrument named is the personal contact and the personal talk with the customer.

The immediate closeness to the customer and the immediate reacting to his wishes cannot only be named as characteristics of the small family businesses under investigation, but they can also be of importance as a market advantage. One of the strengths of the small family businesses under investigation is no doubt the personal and familiar customer relations. To be conscious of this strength and advertise it could contribute to the small family businesses using this market advantage, which sets them off from other companies.

Apart from the personal communication to find out customer wishes, most companies emphasise that experience plays a decisive part in this respect. Experience tells you what the customer has in mind and how to realise his ideas in practice.

Extensive consulting specifies customer wishes and gives the customer the feeling that he is being taken seriously and looked after well.

Regular meetings with the customer, attending specialised fairs/exhibitions, information from specialised journals as well as formalised methods recording of customer wishes (for instance check lists) contribute to completing the knowledge of one's customers and their wishes.

How do customer wishes change?

The combination between product and accompanying services is becoming more important

The companies who are active beyond their own region report of perpetual changes of customer wishes. This applies primarily to the wishes of the customers for newer ranges of products and better design. The allowed time for order processing is becoming tighter for the companies all the time. Everything has to be done faster. The companies, who have a local to regional clientele, report only little change in the wishes of their customers.

Nearly all small family businesses, however, observe changes of customer wishes regards the importance of services beside the actual product. A large demand for "convenient complete solutions" is noted.

> "...What has really changed totally for instance, is the customers' demand for the performance feature "to get everything out of one hand". That didn't use to be the case. There used to be a much more clearly defined segregation between the individual trades, and this tendency is absolutely clear - that is my experience..."
> (Herr Rauen, Baugeschäft Rauen)

> ,,The consulting aspect is increasing all the time. In the past sales took place directly, nowadays everybody has these electronic merchandise systems, that keep the initial purchase of goods relatively low and then they can stock up over the

> system. Therefore the consulting is really important so that the book seller knows, why he actually needs a specific book. The number of pieces is not so important any more so that our position as a salesman has changed. For instance, I carried out downright product schoolings in eight branches for the first time for certain segments, we call that the afternoon market, because we work so closely together with Cornelsen. You see, many parents spend tons of money for the supervision of their children's homework. A lot of money is spent for private coaching schools like Studienkreis, Studienhilfe etc., etc and that is a potential for book sellers, because many children could manage just as well with printed coaching material, which isn't as expensive as coaching lessons. So it's also a case of giving the book sellers a survey of the market to show them new chances where they can prove themselves in order to stabilize their stores."
> (Ewald Mayer, Mayer & Heck GmbH)

The realisation of the service demands gives the companies a chance to open up new possibilities for keeping customers or gaining new customers.

> "We advertise as a service provider doing everything from A-Z, and our customers make use of this willingly."
> (Andreas Conrad, coma GmbH)

> "A new line of business started last year in spring, when one of our customers came to us with the

question whether we couldn't take over the organisation for the dry building jobs, the painting and decorating, flooring as well. The customer wants the burden off his shoulders, he doesn't want anything to do with all that lot and he wants an addressee. We took that up for that particular customer and have since then done this for five other projects, that means we carried out the lighting and alongside made them an offer for the dry building jobs, the painting and decorating and the flooring and carried those jobs out as well ...
...the trend is going towards the customer wanting to talk about everything with us, then he has his peace of mind."
(Herr Goß, Elektro Goß GmbH)

Focus customer wishes

As a central trend the interviewed companies see that the customer wish to be relieved and the demand "to get everything out of one hand" is increasing all the time. The combination of product and services around the product is becoming more important for all companies and is seen by most small family businesses as a chance to keep the regular customers and to gain new customers

> This also applies to the consulting part that the small family businesses have to perform. It is increasing on the whole and opens up a further chance for the companies to excel by good consulting and to survive on the market. The close contact with the customers that most small family businesses have anyway, has a positive effect.
>
> While the "larger" SFBes are confronted with continuous changes of customer wishes in connection with the risen demands to the product and the allowed time for the realisation of commissions by the customers is becoming ever shorter, the "small" SFBes report mainly steady wishes of their customers with little changes.

What importance do ecological materials and production procedures have for customers and small family businesses?

Against the background of a general trend towards more health and environment consciousness we specifically asked the companies about the rating of ecology in their range of products and services.

Are the purchase decisions of the consumers increasingly oriented on the environmental acceptability of the offered product? Can it possibly be a market advantage for small companies to open up to the presumed customer wishes and to take into consideration ecological criteria in the course of production as well as in the choice of materials?

"....I have to point that out to our customers..."

the environmental awareness of the customers as well as the demand for ecologically acceptable products is rather low according to the statements of the interviewed companies.

The Goß company draws their customers' attention to environment-damaging substances as well as products low on energy consumption.

> "It is not adamantly important, but we do mention it. We have a few customers, who do not set great store by that to save money, and we have customers who care very much that old neon light bulbs are not thrown away into the normal household rubbish, but are disposed off environmentally acceptably... That is very important for me."
> (Herr Goß, Elektro Goß GmbH)

At the ecological snack bar the owner reckons that the customers come mainly because of the reasonable lunches and not primarily because it is natural or biological food. One likes to think so, but it is surely not the decisive point. It is different in the field of the natural foods shop. There they have customers, who care particularly for environmentally and ecologically acceptable products.

The coMa company reports that even ecological shops cannot afford material for their stalls at fairs out of natural material and therefore have to refrain from using those.

The Baugeschäft Rauen describes little interest on the part of their customers in e.g. ecological building material.

> "...The little there is, is limited to solvents and substances in glues and tiles/boards, but compared to what is technically possible nowadays and probably coming in the future, this amounts to nothing."
> (Herr Rauen, Baugeschäft Rauen)

> ,,...there simply isn't the knowledge there. You have to consider that the customer is usually a layman. There he is and he wants to do something and perhaps doesn't know, what is possible."
> (Frau Rauen, Baugeschäft Rauen)

First beginnings of an eco-sensitive demand are to be found for instance with the big publishing houses regards the packing material – economic grounds, however, play an equally large part there as ecological.

> "It plays a part for the products, for the topics and for the transport of books, the packing, as little as possible in the way of foil. Large houses like the Mayersche set great store by specific type of

deliveries, that the goods are bundled, that there aren't two tons of rubbish every day and they even ban publishing houses, that cannot fulfil this."
(Ewald Mayer, Mayer & Heck GmbH)

"That is true, but it is also done, because it is cheaper, the handling is cheaper, everything can be disposed of altogether, that's why it plays a role, but ecologically acceptable products are not so important."
(Ulrike Heck, Mayer & Heck GmbH)

Focus ecology

Apart from a few exceptions the companies do not expect a market advantage from the ecologically acceptable products, an ecological service, environmentally acceptable manufacture, etc. SFBes in general react flexibly to the direct demand in the field of ecology from the customers' side. As the demand in the field of ecology is rather small the SFBes often do not regard this field as lucrative.

The differing opinions as to what is ecological, the little demand from the customers' side, the partially inacceptable costs for eco-sensitive material and production procedures as well as the lack of time for acquiring the suitable know-how

> on the part of the small family businesses make the companies - apart from the one, whose identity is based on ecology - refrain from this topic. A trend of customer wishes in this direction is not taken up.

3.1.2.4   Customer contacts

The personal touch counts

We have already been able to determine on asking about the knowledge of customer wishes that the personal talk is decisive. Likewise it becomes apparent in this next chapter that the contact between SFBes and customers is very personal. Just how personal and what importance this has for the customers and the company will be shown in the following.

> *"The relationship is cordial, personal, friendly. People are on first-name terms and aim at a relationship where the customers can identify with the company/shop and are part of it."*
> (Frau Hofen, the Götterspeise company)

The employees and the owners feel part of a large family and this sentiment includes the customers. By the open exchange the customers pick up the occasional internal matter. There has been a donation of 50 Pfennig for the Tax Man. In a family company with two children there are, for instance, conversations with the customers on the upbringing of the children and the small everyday problems, which leads to getting to know more about one another and the relationships with the one or the other customer take on a more private character.

> *"of course there is some gossiping with customers (laughs)"*
> (Herr Golz, the Götterspeise company)

> *„...very personal, because we are a small firm and because everybody is family, this often includes our customers. This goes to the extent that we get invited to birthday parties."*
> (Andreas Conrad, coMa GmbH)

> *"I would say that some customers like my husband very much. He is such a friendly man. He is very endearing and nice and when the customer has some extra wishes, he carries them out and doesn't bill them for that. We have so many long-standing customers that keep ringing us and want my husband to do something for them again. This shows the relationship, that says something for him. There are customers whom my husband has become friends with."*
> (Frau Killat, Killat GmbH)

In the Killat company the boss needs the right "chemistry" between the customer and himself. If that is not ok or there is no understanding, he even does not carry out the work. "When I don't like somebody, he can offer me any price..." (Herr Killat, Killat GmbH).

> "We build up a contact of trust. Most people realise that this is a normal human being coming to see them who has acquired certain skills. The trust arises through giving the occasional piece of advice that doesn't cost anything and saves the customer money. I sometimes get the feeling that that has become rather rare these days."
> (Herr Mörsheim, Mörsheim-Allergieservice)

Because Herr Mörsheim has families with allergy problems as customers, that means a relatively intimate field, it is understandable that consulting families or households has to have a personal understanding character.

> "Immediate contact takes place on the telephone, the personal contact is the exception. It does happen occasionally: on the birth of our third child one customer even came to the hospital to give me a present."
> (Frau Rauen, Baugeschäft Rauen)

Even in this company, where personal contacts mainly take place on the phone according to the company's own statement, the customers tend to show an attitude unimaginable in the relationship with a large company. The relationship structures of the family seem to rub off onto the customers, and presumably this is different for small companies not run by families.

The quotations could be continued in this place, they speak for themselves and on the whole reflect that the contacts of SFBes with their customers are familiar, personal, humane, and trusting.

This is seen as a positive effect of SFBes on the whole and defined as an advantage over other companies.

Focus customer contacts

"You are the cook of my heart"
(a customer to the [female] boss of the Götterspeise company)

Of course this rather nice compliment is rather an exception. It does, however, reflect the satisfaction of the customer with the company and a personal contact on the part of the company to their clientele, which we regard as a typical characteristic of the SFBes.

A noticeable factor in the field of customer satisfaction is the strongly developed understanding of all interviewed companies for customer wishes and customer service which is certainly a consequence of the close contact to the customers. The customer is still "king" in these companies. The contact to the customers is predominantly personal and informal, and certainly goes beyond the pure business contact. This can definitely be called intentional and "normal" in an SFB. The customers get to know internal affairs of the company and family and the people running the companies learn personal matters of their

> customers. The structure of an SFB allows the arising of mutual sympathy and trust. The experience of the SFB under investigation show that many customers want this personal contact and it is seen as an advantage for the company. This makes it possible to commit whole groups of customers to the company over long periods. This is possibly a good approach for advertising if SFBes managed to present this family touch that they describe in their advertising.

3.1.2.5 Advertising

"we wouldn't survive without advertising"

> *"Well, yes, we advertise a lot. There are, first of all, our vans which are full of advertising, and we place a lot of advertisement in the newspapers, we advertise in every regional paper ...well, without advertising, we wouldn't survive."*
> (Frau Killat, Killat GmbH)

For the Killat company advertising in newspapers is the most promising. The vast majority of the customers is in the close vicinity of the company, the district, or bordering districts as well as neighbouring towns. This clientele gets its information on products and services out of the district papers and supplements of the big daily papers. As a company, to whose regular customers count building societies and estate agents who know the work of the Killat company and give them work, it is sensible to advertise for the circle of customers that constitutes the "bread of the company". This is done out of the conviction that the "small customer" is of great importance for the firm and must not be neglected. This attitude can be found in most other companies. It is important to maintain the basis of the clientele and to look after them in many ways. Part of that is surely to give them special personal attention.

> "In our case we try to convey the feeling, "well, yes, I am in good hands there", that is really important. Take the eighty-year-old grandma, who does not know where to go; she is happy to know she can turn to us and that is what the customer ought to feel. We have different aims as self-employed people. In a large company there is often not such a need to be friendly."
> (Frau Rauen, Baugeschäft Rauen)

Apart from the Killat company who advertise a lot in local and supra-local papers and is successful with that, all other firms report that they do not manage to get a lot of custom by advertising in newspapers.

Thank God we do not depend on advertising....

> "...some years ago we placed an advertisement - a larger one in a potential customer organ, the "Haus und Grund" a journal for property owners; with the result that there was

no reaction and we were relieved to notice that we are fortunately not dependent on those advertisements. I wouldn't mind if things stayed that way."
(Herr Rauen, Baugeschäft Rauen)

Question: Do you advertise, do you do any outward representation of your company?

"In principal it would be sensible, we could surely improve business. But as I'm still fully booked at the moment there doesn't seem to be an immediate need."
(Herr Rauen, Baugeschäft Rauen)

,,we have thought about it. It's not as if we are categorically against it, it just hasn't been the right time for it."
(Frau Rauen, Baugeschäft Rauen)

"You have to have some further aims…"
(Herr Rauen, Baugeschäft Rauen)

"We need new perspectives for improvement"
(Frau Rauen, Baugeschäft Rauen)

"I am planning a certain structure long-term, but before that some other things have to be clarified. This concerns our private living-situation, etc., before we proceed, because we cannot get that for peanuts."
(Herr Rauen, Baugeschäft Rauen)

This shows that advertising activities cannot be separated from the private situation at home, from questions of finances, and time problems. "Permanent full-time employment" contributes to the feeling of security and satisfaction, there is no immediate pressure.

Using other media

The partially negative experience made with advertisements in papers led to some companies thinking about other forms of advertising media.

> "...recommendations of the health insurances, new advertising on the vans, and we are trying out various media. We will refrain from the normal advertisements, because they are no use. We will rather go via editorial paths. We are, for instance, developing case studies for the health insurances to show what the health insurance can do for the patients.
>
> (Herr Mörsheim, Mörsheim Allergieservice

The Mörsheim company, which is concerned with allergy problems and has acquired some competence in this field in the course of the years, sees well placed actions as the most effective way of advertising. There is, for instance, a co-operation with medical aid shops, who place advertising boards and offer information for allergic people. The company also has contacts to health insurances who consult patients on allergies and to doctors who draw their patients' attention to the services of the Mörsheim company.

New media are going to be used and a mailing campaign is already under way. A company internet page is to be drawn up in the course of the year 2000. The expected advantage of the medium internet lies in the reduction of the time spent for consulting when the customers are provided with an expressive and informative internet page. The result could be a definite saving of time, which can be made to money, as the consulting took up most of the time in the past.

The internet is becoming of interest to an increasing number of small family businesses

The possibility to advertise in the internet is seen as a perspective for the future and as a service to the customers by most of the interviewed companies and is to be realised by most in the coming year. Two companies do not quite see the advantage for their company and fear that the time spent would be in no proportion to the actual benefit for the company. This is the case at the Götterspeise company and the Killat GmbH. Both have their clientele both locally and regionally and put greater store by mouth-to-mouth advertising. They are not convinced of the effectivity of the internet. Especially the time spent by the owners who then wouldn't be available for the daily running is remarked upon as a hindrance. Comments of friends and customers on the banal character of the internet do not contribute to making the internet more attractive as a possibility for advertising. The ecological snack bar and the natural foods shop, however, with its clientele in the middle class, and that means computer owners, could probably achieve market advantages by the publication of their products and services in the internet.

Homogenous performance

The coMa company tries to present a homogenous performance and targeted advertising in the field of fair/exhibition equipment.

> "We draw up folders, we try to appear in homogenous working clothes, our transport boxes are coloured and bear our inscription, the vans bear our logos. We tried newspaper advertisements, but that didn't work."
> (Andreas Conrad, coma GmbH)

The coMa GmbH sees its "advertising performance" in the context of their "corporate identity", which aims inwards and outwards and reflects the company culture in the outward appearance.

Too much is not good either...

The Elektro Goß GmbH intended to advertise supra-regionally with an image presentation with a large edition (20.000). After the first mailing campaign they were so lucky as to gain several large customers, which have provided full-time employment in the company up to now. There are still 19.950 of those leaflets in the offices of the company. The boss sees that with a fair amount of self-criticism.

> "The background is that we used to work together with a Stuttgart direct-marketing company, where all architects were written; the result was that the first two or three answers were more or less orders; that was so much, that I soon had to say whatever comes now cannot be answered any more. In that case we did the second step before the first."
> (Herr Goß, Elektro Goß GmbH)

More attention by an article in the newspaper

An article in a newspaper about the company is set greater store by than an advertisement. The Götterspeise company reports that an article in the local district supplement of the daily paper led to the shop being crammed with people on the following day and a large resonance even in the week afterwards. Altogether this article had a greater effect than 20.000 flyers which were distributed in the district and in the houses in the past.

The best advertising effect is the mouth to mouth propaganda by satisfied customers

Some companies emphasise the importance of mouth-to-mouth propaganda for them. The Götterspeise company for instance assumes that the best and most successful advertising for them is when the customers recommend the shop to other customers. The same applies to the Prägo-Patrizen company.

> "We get our new customers mainly by mouth-to-mouth propaganda. The only large-scale advertising on our part takes place during the DRUPA."
> (Specialised fair for the printing and paper industry – the author)
> (Frau Grossarth, jun., the Prago-Patrizen company)

This chance to gain sufficient customers by mouth-to-mouth propaganda is, however, strongly linked to the Prägo-Patrizen company working in a market gap without immediate competition and their clientele being very specialised.

When others do the advertising for you

The Mayer & Heck company does not do its own advertising but is recommended in the framework of the advertising of publishing houses as sales representatives which has the advantage that no advertising costs arise for the company.

Focus advertising

Advertising is done by the interviewed companies either very targeted or not at all. Every one of the companies under investigation was of the opinion to have found the adequate type of advertising for themselves. Only one of the companies, though has a thoroughly planned marketing concept (or CI-concept respectively). This is a company that works in advertising itself. The others tackle the advertising issues in a more or less planned manner depending on (competitive) pressure and their own tradition. The more traditional companies that are limited to local areas rely on the traditional forms (advertisements) and personal communication (mouth-to-mouth propaganda); the allergy service which is putting a relatively new service on the market, is developing many ideas for new advertising strategies and media. It is also planning targeted public relations work, which is aiming at the editorial part.

Three companies had already used professional consulting or development of advertising means at some time in the past – in one case with the result to have made the second step before the first.

On the whole all companies under investigation agree, that planned and targeted advertising, not excluding new communication techniques and methods of presentation, will be of increasing importance for the SFBes in the future. The new media will only be interesting for the SFBes under investigation if they save time, do not cost too much and the information seems to make sense for the company. Most SFBes under investigation show a pragmatic view regards the use of advertising media for the company. As a rule only what is deemed necessary happens.

The reason why the companies apart from one exception do not tackle a marketing concept are time and organisational problems. After a 12-14 hour working day as a rule the energy to deal with these problems is usually lacking. Advertising can also be very costly and go beyond the limit of what the SFBes can spend on advertising. A wrong consulting by marketing firms does not contribute to approaching this topic afresh with the help of a competent consulting. A consulting in the field of marketing would have to consider the time, organisational, as well as financial means of the SFBes.

3.1.2 Keyword technology

Owing to the accelerated technological development the products and production procedures differentiate ever faster. The new information and communication techniques (IT, internet, fax, etc.)

are becoming more important and ought to contribute to the company performance.

How do the SFBes handle this development process?

"you cannot survive without fax these days"
(Herr Golz, the Götterspeise company)

With one exception all companies regard their technical equipment (machines, work equipment, tools, vehicles) as not too old, on the current technical level or even one step ahead of the competition.

The Prägo-Patrizen company, which works with an antiquated machine, is still satisfied with the services this machine renders and does not see any need to invest yet.

Some of the investigated companies see additional possibilities and also necessities for investing in the technical field. These are, however, in most cases perspectives for the future.

The Rauen company, for instance, would like to have another van for tools, because the loading of tools and material takes up too much time, and so is too expensive, when there are several sites going at the same time. They also see the need for change in the IT field, as they have been working with a now rather antiquated system for years, a prompt change in this field is not taking place out of lack of time.

"We are thinking of changing our IT equipment, i.e. buy something new. The performance of our computer has to be considered as ancient. The thing is four or five years old. We use Word Perfect as word processing programme, which my wife has modelled to our needs, so that there are some practical screens, I'd like a more specific programme with a shorter work flow and better organisation. What's not very convenient about our IT situation is that we have to leave certain programme parts. You cannot work diagonally. That is easier with new programmes."
(Herr Rauen, Baugeschäft Rauen)

,,There is no time. You have to get to know a system, I am the one who knows the IT better, not the business, but I wouldn't know when to do that. We would have to get to the level that we have now. One has to be able to work that, install a computer. It's not a lack of interest, I am very interested, he is not as interested, but at the moment this isn't possible. We will have to wait another couple of years."
(Frau Rauen, Baugeschäft Rauen)

Mobility plays a decisive role for the Mörsheim company and for the future they plan to service the whole of the Federal Republic of Germany by three to five service-stations with the respective service-vans in the field of allergy consulting.

For the Goß company it is very important to inform themselves of the latest technical development in the electrical trade and beyond and to react to these in order to have the current know-how in the field of new technologies and to make use of the market chances linked with this.

Whereas the technical side plays a rather minor role for the Götterspeise company, and the writing system they use is antiquated (which is not regarded as a disadvantage), the two people running the place do not doubt in the slightest, that they *"would not be able to survive"* without the fax machine, which receives the customers' orders and has become indispensable as a means of communication for the company. They do, however, at this point not see the benefit of the internet and their own homepage. Negative experience of acquaintances of the owners, who have voiced their disappointment about the "fantastic possibilities" of the internet, the assessment, that the time spent would not relate to the success, as well as the little basic knowledge of the possibilities of the internet for companies made them decide not to get involved with this medium for the time being. They regard it as more important to purchase a new professional dishwasher, which takes the washing up off the hands of the employees and so gives them time for new more effective and more profitable tasks.

So there is a weighing up of priorities, where and in what order time and money is invested in technical innovations and the companies then decide in favour of the item that will improve the infrastructure or the running of the business

Technical investments in the field of networking and improvement of the infrastructure or communication structure are of central importance at the Mayer & Heck company.

> *"What we want to invest in is (...) the improvement of the communication ability with G. (their co-operation partner - the author), who has his seat in Hagen, so that we can improve the exchange on the results of our work."*
>
> (Ewald Mayer, Mayer & Heck GmbH)

Internet and email are becoming more important

The new information and communication technologies are important for nearly all companies and in most companies they are in their initial stages or already realised.

The Mörsheim company sees a definite relief and help through a homepage of their own. Customers' requests can be put more precisely on a homepage, which would reduce the high proportion of the consulting time. This would give time for other tasks.

The Prägo-Patrizen company has noted an increased demand of their international clientele since they have been able to communicate through email and internet. After an initial phase of scepticism a homepage for the company is now being developed, which is to contribute to the services of the company being made accessible more easily to the clientele beyond the specialised exhibition taking place every five years.

> *"A year ago I decided to create a homepage for the company. It does not make a good impression on the customer to have to tell him that we are not*

> *available per internet; and once you have started that it is fun."*
>
> (Frau Grossarth jun., the Prägo-Patrizen company)

CoMa expect more information on the topic "fair/exhibition" via an internet connection to be set up in the future. The internet is seen as an up-to-date information exchange and as such it is an interesting factor for the company.

The Elektro Goß company also expects a greater access to information and the respective market by the use of the internet. Herr Goß is convinced that the development is going that way and that the customers expect a presence in the internet.

> *"...You have to be available. We haven't got internet access and email yet, but it is being installed. ...The customer is going to expect that - I am sure of that and I want to provide it. - That is part of the service..."*
>
> (Herr Goß, Elektro Goß GmbH)

An example for the saving of time by the use of information and communication technology.

The Mayer & Heck company, which has the greatest experience with computers, email, internet, ISDN-lines, fax machines, etc. and has been using these instruments for quite a time for their office organisation as well as the communication with their customers speaks of an actual work relief of 10 hours a week by the use of these technologies.

> "We have modelled standard software to our needs for the publishing house representation, so that we have our own data base system for our customer administration, and for the shop we have a merchandise information system, an IT system that we sell to book shops, too, and we have everything we need. Email, fax machine, internet. We need the internet to have a look at the profiles of publishing houses. We are thinking of having our own homepage next year for the publishing house representation as well as the shop."
> (Ewald Mayer, Mayer & Heck GmbH)

Two companies are rather reticent and they can either not see any benefit by the use of the world wide computer net for their company, do not have the necessary time for it or do not want it, because they are *"satisfied with things as they are"*. (Frau Killat, Killat GmbH)

Focus technology

The information and communication technologies are becoming more important for the companies. While the one see it as a service to the customer to be present in the internet and available by email, the others also use the internet as an information exchange and possibility for the presentation of their company.

Most of the companies under investigation state an investment demand in the field of new and further techniques. This applies to new techniques which contributes to improve and facilitate the internal structure of the company (IT, office organisation, etc.) as well as to those with the aim to improve the communication with the customer, the insight into the market, and the image promotion. (Internet, email, etc.)

In order to invest into new techniques the benefit of the techniques has to be definitely apparent and they have to contribute to a short-term relief and improvement of the working situation. As a rule SFBes have the problem, that they have very tight financial and time resources, which means that they have to set priorities.

3.1.3 Keyword economic controlling

The wife often does the bookkeeping

In two thirds of the companies interviewed by us we noted that there is no trained administrative employees.

In the majority of the companies the bookkeeping work is done by the wife in co-operation with a tax consultant.

As a rule the wives have no qualified training as an administrative clerk or in bookkeeping. They have taken over this working field, because all the work like answering the telephone, looking after the customers, administration, and bookkeeping can be combined with the responsibility for housework and upbringing of children.

> "We are a GmbH [Gesellschaft mit beschränkter Haftung = limited liability company – the translator] and I do the office work, plus mother, plus housewife. I do everything around the business, like tax consultant, revenue office. My husband does everything to do with the building site. He looks at the appointments and calculates the prices."
>
> (Frau Killat, Killat GmbH)

In the Mörsheim company the wife is at present attending a qualifying programme for wives working in a SFB. The husband and business partner emphasises the importance of this qualifying for the company. The office has at long last really become an office and the insight into the bookkeeping has improved.

Herr Rauen's wife of Baugeschäft Rauen used to work as a secretary for a large firm and acquired competence there in the handling of customers, Employees management, correspondence, etc. and she can apply this favourably in their company.

Most owners have acquired experience in bookkeeping by "learning by doing". Two of the interviewed companies have trained and qualified Employees for this field.

Despite the fact that the majority of companies do not have qualified personnel for the bookkeeping the companies seem to have the bookkeeping in order.

There is only one SFB with a performance controlling

"Controlling" means those controlling instruments which a company possesses to manage the business. The more refined these instruments, the more flexible, faster, and more efficient the management can react for instance to a change in the order situation, new competitive situation or other changes of the business situation."[7]

All interviewed companies have their bookkeeping up to date so that an economic assessment is largely possible.

---

[7] Dahle, G., Schrader, M., controlling for small companies and service enterprises – project report, Bochum, 1998, p. 4

Where there is a performance controlling system, the owner-managers report, that this is a very sensitive issue to decide how and at what point to start with such systems in the company and emphasise the importance of the conveyance to the employees.

> "...This is a highly delicate issue to install such a system. We do some controlling: we assess projects, we give out a calculation beforehand which is binding."
> (Andreas Conrad, coMa GmbH)

For coMa GmbH it is extremely important to install an effective system in the field of actual costing of customer orders. For the establishment of the real costs it was essential for the employees to note the occurred work and the respective working time.

The controlling-system caused fears in its introductory phase: fear of increased work pressure, sanctions, etc., as a consequence employees undermined the system. Once the economic reasoning behind the work time recording was brought home to the employees, and the system was simplified, the acceptance of the system was higher.[8]

The fact that coMa works with a controlling system is due to two factors:

- the immediate economic necessity of an effective actual costing

---

[8] cp. Project report to . coMa in: ibid.

- the eagerness for innovations on behalf of the owners

None of the other companies works with controlling systems.

Controlling is good, trusting is better

"For work time controlling I rely on my mechanics to be honest and fair, we are, too, we pay in excess of the (collectively agreed) scale, have other fringe benefits, which we pay out to the mechanics. For the calculations for a finished site, I do that by instinct: material roughly estimated, the hours, that we have to work out for the wage calculations, are added up and multiplied, and that all has to work out and as a rule it does... I am not very particular. When I get a new customer, that gives me two hundred marks. Controlling is not worth it, because everything is still lucid."

(Herr Goß, Elektro Goß GmbH)

"I take a look at what the employees show me, - I am the controlling authority and I say: "Stop, that needs rework" or "that's ok" – I can't be everywhere at the same time and that is not the point. There is a relationship of trust there. That is of elementary importance to me; when I can't trust people any more, then there is no point. If it turned out that I have to have doubts, then I would

probably let go of that employee. That would be a reason to rethink seriously."

(Herr Rauen, Baugeschäft Rauen)

Focus controlling

The SFBes have a lack of trained administrative employees, but according to their own statement this does not result in having no insight in the bookkeeping or the economic situation. In most cases the wives keep the books, and they have usually taught themselves.

The majority of the companies do not use any formalised forms of work time or quality controlling, on the one hand because the boss takes over the controlling personally in a small company, on the other hand because one feels that such controlling systems express distrust towards the Employees.

Trusting the employees is an elementary part of the culture of the SFBes. A lot works on the basis of mutual trust, and that is desired by both sides, owners and employees or rather described as essential for SFBes. Looking at the answers of both the interviewed employees and the owners this fact makes for a good atmosphere in the company.

Whether a performance and quality controlling makes sense for an SFB depends among other factors upon its size (how many sites can a boss look after simultaneously?) and the work processes. (how many places do the employees work at?). Many owners of small companies probably do not know much about the possibilities and effects of controlling systems, i.e. they do not know much about alternatives to the direct personal controlling by the boss.

When a decision is come to in favour of controlling, it is essential to include the employees in the development and to convey the purpose, so that the system is not understood as a "breach of trust" and is supported by the employees.

3.1.5 Keywords employees and management style

A company is as good as its employees

Motivation and commitment of the employees are decisive factors for the effectivity, performance, and quality of a company. Team and personnel development models bank on employees, who can think and take on responsibility. This presupposes that they are given responsibility and that the business proceedings are transparent for all participants.

Expectations to the employees

Concerning the expectations to the employees there are differing demands and wishes on the side of the interviewed companies. The largest agreements are regards the demands for identification with the company, working fast and well, honesty, not off sick too often, working independently and being open-minded.

> "They do have to be flexible, they have to work independently, have to be circumspect, must have motivation."
> (Frau Grossarth jun., Prago-Patrizen)

> "They have to be dependable; insofar as they should be more or less punctual. The odd quarter of an hour is ok, but that should be all. Honesty,

loyalty to me, doing their work thoroughly the way I told them to do it and to do things my way when we have not spoken about a job. They ought to know how I want a job done and that they stick to that, a kind of quality controlling."
(Herr Rauen, Baugeschäft Rauen)

"I expect the students in the shop to work independently. They have to have a little experience of life."
(Frau Heck, the Mayer & Heck company)

"that they don't stay off sick too often, because a small firm cannot afford that; that they do their work well, so that we don't get too many complaints."
(Frau Killat, Killat GmbH)

"Employees should like their work, know the rights and duties of an employee – work does not consist of earning money alone -, and enjoy their work. I want to have a family business. Not with a hierarchical system, but with a round table. I am open for comments. If somebody has a good idea, it is listened to, thought about and realised. I expect performance and am then prepared to pay accordingly."
(Herr Mörsheim, Mörsheim Allergieservice)

How much do the employees know about the company?

Apart from two companies, where only one employee knows about the financial situation of the company, the other companies report, that their employees know everything about the company regarding the work and the customers, but are kept out of the financial matters.

> "The employee who does the bookkeeping, knows about the financial situation of the company, of course. The other employees have no insight into the finances."
> (Frau Grossarth jun., the Prägo-Patrizen company)

> "They can know a lot about the business procedure, but there are certain things that are none of their business, for instance the calculation, the bookkeeping. When somebody starts to work for me, that gives me a great responsibility. He has a family to feed like me; so a certain amount of trust has to be built up. I want to employ people long-term, not for a year or two. I want them to identify with the company, I want them to bring in ideas, and then they are motivated and really work. That is good for me too."
> (Herr Mörsheim, Mörsheim Allergieservice)

> „They get to know the orders position. When I get orders in, I let them know that. "We will start at such and such place soon." — I try to involve them and give them responsibility. I don't want them to

just receive their orders in the morning, I want them to make their own solution proposals or act independently."

(Herr Rauen, Baugeschäft Rauen)

"Only my nephew (knows about everything. the author), the other two are kept out of things, it is none of their business, they don't have to know too much."

(Frau Killat, Killat GmbH)

The small size and the familiar working situation create a natural transparency in a lot of the business processes. This transparency stops at the finances. It is probably no coincidence that the prevailing attitude, that employees do not have to know everything, reminds of traditional patriarchal family structures.

Transparency of the finances in a family company means simultaneously the opening up of the financial situation of the family – so the barrier is understandable.

Job perspectives of the employees

In the majority of companies the question of the job perspective of the employees in the company was answered positively insofar as the job, as far as one can tell, will not be lost. In two of the companies this does not apply for all employees. Career perspectives, and so an improvement of the working situation, were only thinkable among the "large ones among the small companies" in the case of an expansion of the company.

> "We try to offer our employees a perspective in every respect, to show them the whole spectrum of exhibition building, so that they can work in all parts of the job, we do not have a specialist for every field. We let them participate in the preparation phase... With these buildings we have the chance to increase our capacity. We could work with 30 people here, that is a perspective. Because the people that work here now, would have managing positions if we took on more people."
> (Andreas Conrad, coma GmbH)

Question: do the employees in your company have a career perspective?

> "Yes, I would say so. We do not train. My nephew wasn't in the company, where he was officially doing his apprenticeship, for more than a year out of the three years' apprenticeship. We cannot afford that. We can only employ somebody who brings in money, for whom we don't have to pay. Apprentices should go to bigger companies, it doesn't matter so much there, if one person doesn't work so much. A small company depends on everybody."
> (Frau Killat, Killat GmbH)

> *"No, they don't have a career perspective in my firm."*
> (Frau Grossarth, the Prägo-Patrizen company)

There are hardly any professional perspectives in the sense of a career in the companies. The companies, that are going to expand, might be able to offer a career and in those, where the next 10 to 20 years are thought about, reflections are taking place, that employees could probably become foremen or the "boss' s right hand". On the whole things do not look too good for employees here.

Only very few companies offer their employees the chance of training or qualifying programmes outside the firm. On the one hand there is a lack of knowledge of adequate possibilities and offers, and also there is obviously only little to no demand on the side of the employees. An important reason why one hasn't bothered sufficiently about this, is again the lack of time.

Promotion of motivation

Nearly all companies try to increase their employees' motivation by personal talks and attention. This relates to company as well as to private matters. Praise and appreciation for the work performed play a minor role according to them. Parties as well as company fringe benefits were named twice. Everybody seems to know that the employees need a lot of care and attention, especially when they are away a lot for the company. Proposals for improvements by the employees are described as positive and are desired. The employees' answers prove, that it is possible to contribute, that you are listened to and that real changes do result from those proposals.

> *"I have to regard them as human beings, be open for their instigations and give them the feeling, that they are a part of the whole. They must not be the valve for my moods."*
> (Herr Mörsheim, Mörsheim-Allergieservice)

> *,,...for motivation I have following topics: What can I earn? What does the company have to offer in the way of social contributions? What does the company do for my pension? We have taken out a company pension scheme for the employees, which was received very positively - everybody has joined it. Apart from that the work climate has to be right. When I notice personal problems I try to talk about them and help where I can."*
> (Herr Goß, Elektro Goß GmbH)

Criticism on the part of the employees

Criticism on the part of the employees, and this applies especially to constructive criticism, is desired and encouraged. Three owners remark, that they do not find it easy to be criticised. But when the criticism is justified, they try to deal with it positively.

"I can handle it and keep on asking for it. That usually comes in the form of a proposal for improvement. Sometimes an employee just hasn't been well enough informed, why a decision was come to in a certain way. Then I explain it and I want to hear criticism in the future."
(Herr Goß, Elektro Goß GmbH)

"I can handle justified criticism quite well. Criticism has to be sound. That is the problem with most companies, that the boss criticises things of which the employees know that he can't do them himself."
(Herr Mörsheim, Mörsheim Allergieservice)

Question: How do you handle criticism by the employees?

"Nobody dares criticise me (he laughs). When it is constructive criticism I am grateful for it. Nobody likes to be criticised, but that usually sets a discussion going on the topic and usually a clever solution. At least the topic is handled beforehand, before it is realised."
(Herr Rauen, Baugeschäft Rauen)

Focus employees

The company owners want responsible and independently working employees for their companies. They want employees who are reliable, work well and can identify with the company. The only slight fluctuation in the interviewed companies - with one exception - speaks for the fact that a satisfying employment situation for both sides has been created. For the employees it is important, that they can identify with the work situation and feel that they are in good hands in the SFB, that they feel understood and accepted.

In the field of job perspectives for the employees there is a critical point: promotion prospects are difficult to realise or not available. That this has no negative effect on the motivation of the employees is demonstrated by the fact that all the interviewed employees are prepared to take on responsibility beyond their usual scope and, for instance, stand in for their bosses in case of illness.

The employees are only seldom informed about the financial situation and when they are, it is only because they are employed for the bookkeeping in the company or belong to the family. Although little is talked about the financial situation of the company, this does not apply to the processing of the orders, the customer contacts as well as all the work in the companies. There is a large interest in those fields for the employees to be able to understand the contexts of the company and so be in the position to contribute independent thinking and work.

On behalf of the companies the promotion of the employees' motivation is undertaken in various ways. The personal conversation with the employees is thought to be the most important instrument in this respect. But additional fringe benefits for the employees, company parties, and encouragement in the case of proposals for improvement contribute to the increase of motivation. Criticism is not only desired and regarded as a positive factor, but in several cases it is deliberately encouraged by the company owners.

Both the interviewed employees and the company owners regarded the motivation of the Employees as very high. This can be attributed both to the personal relationship of most employees with the boss and to the family situation in the company.

> *"We know each other personally, had known one another, before I started here, that's how I ended up here. It is a mixture. Of course we have a business relationship, but it is something like a friendship, although we see each other rarely or not at all outside the company. This mixture leads to the connection with the company becoming closer, it creates responsibility. I have often felt as if it were my business."*
> (a female employee of the Prägo-Patrizen company)

Communication and management style

The quality of the internal communication in the company contributes largely to the efficiency and quality of the working processes in the company. A functioning communication creates transparency and promotes the effectivity of teamwork; a management style of "low hierarchies" supports the identification and motivation of the employees. Whether and how such principles of "modern management" manifest in small family businesses we have questioned under the aspects teamwork, communication structures, and management style.

"You cannot call that teamwork"

The question whether there is teamwork in the companies was answered very similarly by company owners and employees alike. The following answer is typical:

> "You cannot call that teamwork, but nobody just works by himself. The work is distributed, but there is a certain amount of mixing, i.e. we were in constant touch... We have supported one another."
> (female employee at the Prägo-Patrizen company)

Most companies do not talk about teamwork themselves. There are work foci for the individual employees and these are employed according to their qualifications and training.

> "We have focal points in that direction, for example: An employee who knows module building like windows and doors, fitting work like locks; another is competent in the coarser work like roughcasting, mason work, the third has the know-how in dry building, and all three together can do several other jobs. The stucco worker for instance can also do dry building. That overlaps."
> (Herr Rauen, Baugeschäft Rauen)

All companies speak of teamwork in the everyday sense of the word., that means that they all support each other and sometimes have to take over somebody else's work.

> "There is no other way sometimes. We help each other. When the carpenter has more to do, we all do woodwork. And the other way round in this sense teamwork. We do not withdraw entirely to our own work and professional fields."
> (employee at coMa GmbH)

Working together and a high flexibility of the employees have a high rating in the SFBes under investigation. This corresponds on the one hand with the personal work climate, which is part of the company structure, on the other hand the size of the company often demands that the working fields not be strictly separated.

Communication structures

Working sessions take place in the two businesses that have more Employees and relatively large commissions or where the employees do not meet every day because they are away on construction jobs. These working sessions do not, however, take place once a week.

> "We meet three times a year to speak about internal matters. For acute problems like the supervision of the work on a site, is somebody going to take over the job or do I name somebody, and with that person I meet up, on a Saturday in general to speak about the site. When something has been forgotten, we speak on the telephone."
> (Herr Goß, Elektro Goß GmbH)

> "There are meetings depending on the season. There are times when there are hardly any meetings with the employees, but at other times they are more often"
> (Andreas Conrad, coMa GmbH)

Informal structures like on-the-quiet information and notes as well as meetings when there is a topical problem are the predominantly practised forms of communication in the investigated businesses.

> "When I was still working full-time here, we had no particular structure for that, because we saw one another every day. We made the arrangements, when we just happened to meet and something

> *was acute. We had no fixed dates. Those were only made when extraordinary things had to be talked about."*
> (a female employee at Prägo-Patrizen)

> *"The employees either inform each other, write notes or sometimes ring each other up."*
> (Frau Grossarth jun., the Prägo-Patrizen company)

The meetings which took place regularly at the beginning were given up in the course of the development of the businesses due to lack of time and demand.

> *"...in the beginning (there were work meetings, the author), but somehow that sorted itself out. I see the boss at the change of shifts at 16.30 hours, we talk about everything on the agenda, I ask or there is a note for me. Otherwise I know what to do... apart from that we've been friends for ten years. So we talk a lot privately about the shop."*
> (employee at the Götterspeise company)

Management style

The management style in most of the businesses is described as "relaxed" and "matey", which does not exclude getting clear directions. We were also told of conflicts between wanting to be co-operative and authoritarian practice:

> Question: How would you describe your management style?

> *"That depends. There are things where I act authoritarian, but I try to include the employees. I think they have to show responsibility to be able to create a satisfactory work situation."*
> (Herr Rauen, Baugeschäft Rauen)

> *„He likes to delegate and is disappointed afterwards when it doesn't really succeed. They would have the chance to take on more responsibility, to do things more independently - and then he notices that it is not really working that way and then he has to authoritarian again."*
> (Frau Rauen, Baugeschäft Rauen)

> *„It is a different way of thinking. That is almost the nature of the matter. I talk with the colleague who has started his own garden and landscaping business. As a self-employed person and as the one, who is responsible for the whole lot and has to answer for it you see everything with different eyes. I have the overall view, and the employee only sees a little part of it. He only sees his work detail and does not see the whole context."*
> (Herr Rauen, Baugeschäft Rauen)

It would be interesting to probe into the background of such experience. You would probably find, that there are possibilities for developing the desired independence of the employees. Or that we have here the type of employee who does not like taking on responsibility.

Bosses have to be bosses sometimes; despite a co-operative management styles - at least the employees see it that way:

> Question: how would you describe the management style?
>
> *"Very co-operative, very understanding, sometimes not enough of a boss, when it comes to getting things done the way she wants them done."*
> (female employee at the Prägo-Patrizen company)

Two different management styles

> *"I don't regard my style as boss not as a boss, but rather as a colleague. I do not think of myself as a person who is above everything."*
> (Frank Conrad, coMa GmbH)

> *"Of course one likes to make things as nice as possible. You have to give clear instructions, when you discuss things the result is rubbish. You come into conflict, because you make the decisions as the boss, there is no discussion, that is done as I want it done; but that is important, because it is then tangible for the employees."*
> (Andreas Conrad, coMa GmbH)

They are **the** managing team in the company, but it is clear, that they define their management style differently.

When you consider the differing work places of the two cited brothers in the company, it is easier to understand the statements. Frank Conrad is responsible for production and is often on the road with the fitters, whereas Andreas Conrad looks after the organisational side of the business, the billing, the acquisition, as well as the customer service.

It is remarkable that the employees have learned to handle the differing approaches and that both are possible alongside one another.

Management is a "question of personality"

> "That is a question of the personality of both of us, as we both have the fate of the business in our hands. We do not have a division of competencies now, but Ewald is a person who is very creative in his work and he can produce new ideas all the time, that is not my way…the management style towards the employees that is my job, I say how we are going to handle the students, I have to show them the job, too."
>
> (Ulrike Heck, Mayer & Heck GmbH)

Focus management style

Even though no teamwork in the closest sense of the word can be found in the investigated SFBes, team spirit, a sense of togetherness, and various forms of co-operation see to it, that people feel a team in the business.

Prepared and regular working sessions are not to be found in the FFBs investigated by us. Only the "larger ones among the small ones" have something like work sessions – though often with big time gaps. Nearly all businesses started with regular work sessions, but nowadays situative meetings and sessions, notes as well as information passed on the phone between the employees are predominant. The better the company functions the less work sessions are deemed necessary. According to the companies production or other work processes do not suffer from this in the slightest.

The management style or rather the management styles of the owners distinguish themselves insofar that they state that they do largely without authoritarian measures. The majority of the owners of the SFBes want the management to take place in an exchange with the employees. The management style of the various owners are mainly set apart by their personalities. Management consisting of orders to the employees is declined and not practised by all interviewed companies. – It seems that in some cases the bosses would like would like the hierarchy to be lower, the employees value the friendly contact with the boss, but still would rather have a clear management attitude.

3.2 SPECIAL FEATURES OF THE SMALL FAMILY BUSINESSES

Between emotional ties and economic demands

A decisive characteristic of the small family business (SFB) is the overlapping and interacting of two social systems, family and business.

Whereas the family relies on emotions, protection, care, love, and human relations, the company has to follow the free market laws and satisfy demands like productivity, effectivity, growth, cost reduction, etc.

The special feature of the SFB is therefore first of all their belonging to two different social systems, which they have to combine. The following part of the investigation, which deals with the interaction of family and business, is to clarify, how the investigated SFB manage that, and where the chances and risks lie between these two systems.

3.2.1 Relationship family – business

The family flat is also the office

In the investigated SFBes business and family usually form a union, merely because of the vicinity of company premises and living quarters of the family.

SMALL. FAMILY. BUSINESSES.

Half the investigated businesses have their office rooms in their family flat. Here the everyday life of administration and office work as well as partially the customer consulting takes place along with the housework and upbringing of the children.

At the time of the investigation one of the owners was still living in a flat integrated in the premises of the company.

> "As long as coMa has existed I have always had the office in my flat directly opposite. I will now move away from the business for the first time and put a distance between me and the business. Up to now I have always been present and had close family contact despite the long working hours. The consequence is of course, because my wife also works in the company, that family and company cannot be separated because of living so close and working together."
> (Andreas Conrad, coma GmbH)

Herr Goß of Elektro Goß GmbH has had new premises built in Welver next to his house, which can be used multi-functionally for the business now and as a block of flats later on. At the moment the workshop and the store-room is on the ground floor, the offices, the conference rooms, and the reception rooms for the customers on the first floor.

The Götterspeise company has a small room for the office work on the business premises and belongs to those SFBes, along with the Prägo-Patrizen company that have the most distinct division between company and family quarters.

SMALL. FAMILY. BUSINESSES.

"Family and company are one, you cannot really differentiate there."
(Herr Mörsheim, Mörsheim-Allergieservice)

On the whole the business plays a large role in the families. It determines the everyday rhythm and has a strong effect on family life.

> *"The family lives with the business. The family is confronted with the business all day long."*
> (Frau Killat, Killat GmbH)

> *Family and business are one, you can't really differentiate there. At any rate, the highs and lows of the last years have welded us together."*
> (Herr Mörsheim, Mörsheim-Allergieservice)

> Question: What rating does the communication about the business in the family?

> *"The business always plays a role. It has increased since we've moved the office to our flat. Before when we had separate premises we at least had our peace from 21.00 hours onwards."*
> (Ewald Mayer, Mayer & Heck GmbH)

> *"My wife does want to know what's happening the positive and the negative happenings. But when I get home at night, I don't always feel like talking about business matters. The exchange about business matters could be better. That is because

she doesn't always have time, when I happen to be at home because of the two kids for instance and I sometimes just don't feel like talking about it in the evening. That could be better."
(Herr Goß, Elektro Goß GmbH)

"It's not as if we talk about things all the time, but I do talk about what's happened."
(Herr Rauen, Baugeschäft Rauen)

„The first question at night is always the day's turnover and the more that's been the better the mood. We probably tell each other the one or other story, but then it's enough about the business. Switching off is important, talking about other things and dreaming too. It was important from the start to keep the weekend free. We see one another in the shop every day, but we have little outside activities."
(Herr Golz, the Götterspeise company)

"The business doesn't have the same rating in the family situation any more. Nowadays we only rarely talk about the business in private. That was different in the beginning, of course."
(Frau Grossarth jun., the Prägo-Patrizen company)

The business topics, the negative and positive events, play a decisive role in the family and belong to the every day life of the family. Whereas most families manage to not talk exclusively about the business and let their lives be determined by it, the majority of the families live in the tension field between family and business. Depending of the attitude of the respective persons this is described as a strain or as a "normal state of affairs".

> "That's the way it is in a family business"
> (Frau Killat, Killat GmbH)

The time spent for the business is above-average high.

In most businesses the husbands work far more than 50 hours a week and have been doing this for more than 50 years.

> "You can say fifteen hours a day, Saturdays ten, a bit on Sundays too, about ninety hours a week."
> (Herr Goß, Elektro Goß GmbH)

> "Every free minute, until we get a headache. Between twelve and sixteen hours a day during the week. The weekend is reserved for the cars; I tidy up the office and do the housework. I'm trying to introduce a more effective time management."
> (Herr Mörsheim, Mörsheim-Allergieservice)

> "Around sixty to eighty hours, but it varies. Regularly ten hours a day and it has peaks. Every Saturday and Sunday is effected in some way or other."
> (Herr Rauen, Baugeschäft Rauen)

> *„Twenty-four hours a day. Always. I answer the phone up to 10 p.m. at night and talk to customers. We don't have an answering machine, because I don't like talking on an answering machine myself either. We are available for the customers till late at night."*
>
> (Frau Killat, Killat GmbH)

At the Götterspeise company the share of wife's working hours, who works in the business about 60 hours a week, is about 10 hours more than the husband's. this has to do with the internal division of labour in the business and with the fact that the husband takes over more of the housework and the upbringing of the children.

Only at Mayer & Heck and at Prägo-Patrizen, where the owners have defined it as their aim to work less, do the owners manage to limit their weekly working hours to fifty hours. They both emphasise, however, that this has only recently changed and that they worked a lot more hours at the beginning of their self-employment.

Although the men work for the business far more than fifty hours a week, and so more than their wives, the women mostly underestimate their working time and the share that they do for the business. To the question about the working time there came assessments like "a few hours" up to about 25 hours a week, apart from Frau Killat who says that she is on call for the business twenty-four hours a day. A closer look, however, shows far longer working hours, when you count the permanent readiness for instance answering the phone, talking to customers, enquiries, orders, etc., and above all when you include the work that women perform for the family in the house and looking after the children so that the husband can devote his time to the business. This high input for business and family is recognised by the husbands and the importance of the wife working for the business is in no way denied.

> "Even though she doesn't work here a lot, it is very high (the share of the work, the author), because the husband is seldom at home. There has to be a nail driven into the wall or a drain cleaned, things a woman does rather rarely otherwise. Insofar she does her share of the work for the business. It's not only her work, but where the man in the family is missing."
> (Herr Goß, Elektro Goß GmbH)

On the whole the working hours and the performance for a family business cannot be compared with wage-earning employees. They are considerably higher. When you count the evening conversations about the business in the family and the answering of customer requests sometimes later than 22.00 hours and at the weekend, you can understand more fully Frau Killat's statement:

> "We are available for our customers 24 hours a day."
> (Frau Killat, Killat GmbH)

The obligation of tradition

Most of the owners come from families of self-employed and hardly question their working situation. Generally they say, that self-employed people do as a rule have to work more than other people. So this attitude results on the one hand from the tradition in the families and on the other hand it corresponds to the high demands put to self-employed people nowadays.

> "…we both come from families where the fathers were self-employed and we just don't know it any different. I used to work normally, but I am not the type to drop the hammer at five o'clock. Even as an employee I was someone who used to work overtime without writing down the extra time. That means someone every employer likes to have."
> (Frau Rauen, Baugeschäft Rauen)

We can't really afford to be ill

Most of the interviewed owners are aware that the situation would not be easy to manage, if one of them fell ill. Whereas some have made provisions for such a situation insofar as one of their friend or the professional field would stand in, other businesses would be in a predicament should a longer absence occur.

Question: If one of you fell ill, could the business carry on?

"That depends on how long for. We haven't got a stand-in, the positions in the business are too extreme for that. If M.(a family employee from the office, the author) is ill for a week, there is a huge gap."
(Andreas Conrad, coMa GmbH)

"If one of us were absent, although it would be a lot more difficult, if Nicole were absent, it could just possibly go on. If both were absent, the shop definitely couldn't go on, neither employees-wise nor finances-wise."
(Herr Golz, the Götterspeise company)

"We'd have to try. My nephew is quite a hard worker, we could trust him, he is always there for us. We'd have to try to build the business around him. We wouldn't go bankrupt, but it would be bad."
(Frau Killat, Killat GmbH)

"It might be possible, probably even for six months. Because of the co-operation that we've just entered our new partner there could take on some work for us. Apart from that there is a lot of solidarity among the representatives, so that another representative could carry on our work. We always help each other out in our sector."
(Ewald Mayer, Mayer & Heck GmbH)

"I don't get sick. (he laughs). No, I was once and the business carried on. I have a good circle of friends and acquaintances that stands in then for the business. The business is and will be so designed that it will always be able to carry on even if something bad happened to me."
(Herr Mörsheim, Mörsheim-Allergieservice)

The work together with the members of the family is described as good and necessary

The co-operation of the family members in the business is described as important and good. A high amount of reliability resulting from family ties is considered as a special advantage.

"We work together well. Everybody has a bad day sometimes, but our co-operation is good."
(Frau Killat, Killat GmbH)

Basic decisions concerning family and business are made together

Most people in the investigated businesses stated that basic decisions both in the family and in the business are made together, even though the responsibilities are otherwise clearly defined in the various fields of family and business.

"The important decisions for the family, but also for the business are, of course, made together. Many small decisions, like the children's matters or factual work decisions are made by those who are concerned with them."
(Herr Rauen, Baugeschäft Rauen)

„We decide that together. There are things she decides on her own; you know that by instinct, the matters you don't have to ask your partner about, but the decisive situations we do together."
(Herr Goß, Elektro Goß GmbH)

"I do everything to do with finances, my husband brings in the money."
(Frau Killat, Killat GmbH)

Risks and chances for the family and the business are close together

Some of the owners state clearly that the family gets a bad deal and that the children in particular suffer when mother and father do not have any time for them.

"I look after the children. They do get a bad deal, though. I must say I don't have enough time for the children. They have everything in the way of material things, but that is not everything."
(Frau Killat, Killat GmbH)

> "When you consider that I am on the road 26 days a month, so I don't have any time for the family."
> (Frank Conrad, coMa GmbH)

> "The family suffers, of course, the children too. I sometimes feel sorry for the children, but life in Germany has become so dammed expensive. I have not yet noticed that families with three children have become better off in Germany. Being able to feed my family comes first for me. But there are also nice sides, I have seen the kids grow up. Which man can say that. I was always at home. You can combine the personal and business matters well at home."
> (Herr Mörsheim, Mörsheim-Allergieservice)

Additionally ten to fifteen hours work a day and that up to seven days a week over a period of ten years or longer play havoc with the body and the health suffers.

> "I hope that the business will be able to carry on as long as my husband can work. I don't want him to retire at sixty-five. He'll not last that long. I want him to stop working at fifty, that the business will carry on till then, then we can pay everything off by then and be able to put a bit aside."
> (Frau Killat, Killat GmbH)

The families have "*gone through thick and thin together*" (Herr Mörsheim, Mörsheim-Allergieservice), which has moulded them together and can be taken as their strength. Working together for the business also has a positive effect on the family and contributes to an identity with the business.

> *"From time to time it is certainly a burden, that we talk so much about the business, but that is our common interest, which ties us together. It is a part, to have something in common and to create something together achieves a common identity."*
> (Ulrike Heck, Mayer & Heck GmbH)

> *"I used to work as a foreign correspondence secretary and do work today that is really not qualified enough for me, but I enjoy it, because it is, after all, for ourselves."*
> (Frau Rauen, Baugeschäft Rauen)

> *„We had to make a decision this year, therefore it was a very, very difficult year. We decided at the beginning of the year to put all our eggs in one basket. Before that I was doing a lot of things on my own, that got on top of me eventually, there are still things left to catch up on. At some point you just can't do everything on your own any longer, you then either have to it together and join forces or you go under and will always stay the small-timer that you were."*
> (Herr Mörsheim, Mörsheim-Allergieservice)

Whereas there is the danger of the personal relationships being neglected by spending a lot of the energy, the time together and the conversations in the family on business topics, there is on the other hand the big chance for a specially close togetherness in the family arising out of the joint link with the business.

This close relationship of business and family does bear a risk, though. In the case of a crisis in the business this can have a negative effect on the family or even break up a family. A crisis in the marriage or a divorce can conversely have a grave effect on the continuation of the business.

3.2.2 Objectives of small family businesses

Economic security

All interviewed owners name as top priority for objectives for the family and the business, that they want to live in financial security. In this context most other interviewed owners want sufficient turnover for their business, that serves to cover all costs, maintain the living standard of the family, that there are no changes for the worse and the personal wishes of the family can be fulfilled. The financial aims for the business always have an immediate context with the life plans and the aims of the family.

Only one of the interviewed owners gave precise financial targets for the business in the way of turnover figures for the coming year.

"Earn so much that all costs are covered, all employees can be paid and what is left over for living."
(Frau Killat, Killat GmbH)

"That we can live well from our work, that the business is not in the red, which seems to look good this year and that we always have enough. That doesn't have to be millions."
(Herr Mörsheim, Mörsheim-Allergieservice)

,,Short-term, that all outstanding bills may be paid, and that we get the money from our customers faster (after the work is finished, of course). They are not very fast in paying their bills. Long-term: That the financing of the firm's new premises will work out, that we can pay the loans, that means that we have enough work, keep our regular customers, and that we become millionaires."
(laughs)
(Andreas Conrad, coma GmbH)

That is difficult to answer in general. First of all, of course, to make as much money as possible, because that's why we are doing all this. Seeing it philosophically, there are only a limited number of years in which we can do this and then that's it. Therefore we try to get good prices and to lose as little of the potential profit by working efficiently."
(Herr Rauen, Baugeschäft Rauen)

> „The year 1999 brought an increase in turnover of 30% and we mean it to increase it by 30% again in 2000. This is already nearly certain, as there are already 30 more orders for shop building this year than 1999. The objective for the business is therefore an increase in turnover of 30% in 2000.
> (Herr Goß, Elektro Goß GmbH)

Less work, more time for the family and more relief

Next to the important point of the safeguarding of their existence the wish for more time for the family is in second place followed by the wish for relief in the business so that they don't have to work so much any more as well as the wish to give the kids good preconditions for the start into their future.

> "To remain economically independent. We are wealthy enough. Our profit maximising is to take the shape, that we get down from the long working hours, but the earnings stay the same. Therefore we always have to acquire new customers. But beyond that we are quite happy with our level. The objective is clear: to have more time for the family.
> (Herr Mayer, Mayer & Heck GmbH)

> "For the family more success for the business would mean more turnover, more turnover means more profit, therefore more work could be delegated and more time be left over for the family. Another objective is not to work Saturdays

or Sundays any longer and maybe go on holiday twice a year."
(Herr Mörsheim, Mörsheim Allergieservice)

„Objective for the family: Getting old without quarrelling, without stress, to lead a harmonious life. I have to contribute my share. That can take place by my intention to employ "a right hand" next year. That will give me more time to spend with my family and be more balanced.
(Herr Goß, Elektro Goß GmbH)

"The size and the setting of the business is to remain and continue going well. On top of that I would like to delegate and organise a bit more. For my private life I'm hoping for more relief, also from the new employee and I would like to have another leg to stand on."
(Frau Grossarth jun., Prägo-Patrizen)

"That things go well for us, that we can lead a good life. For me that doesn't mean buying an expensive car or a mink coat, but we do not want to live from hand to mouth. It is important to us that our kids get a good start in life"
(Frau Rauen, Baugeschäft Rauen)

„The aim would be a second economically independent shop, and that we wouldn't have to work so much any longer, be able to live of the money well, that the kids would have no

disadvantages through the shop and we could have the washing machine repaired."
(Frau Hofen, the Götterspeise company)

Modest objectives and wishes for the family

The objectives of the SFBes for the business and family can be regarded as modest. The primary financial objective of the investigated SFBes is not to make short-term profits, but to maintain and expand the achieved economic status, to minimise risks, and to secure the family income.

The business is to make a higher turnover in the longer run and still give the security to lead a financially carefree life. Whereas one SFB was able to name an actual increase of turnover for the coming year, the others want to "make enough to cover the costs" and be able to "live well" of the work. The financial objectives are the most important and were named first.

The business objectives are closely linked with what the family needs and what one wants for oneself. Business objectives are often secondary to family planning and a new place to live for the family has a higher priority than e.g. the presence of the business in the internet.

More time for the family and less work takes second place. Some businesses work specifically towards that aim and want to achieve relief by a co-operation with other businesses from the sector as well as by employing new Employees. Others voice this as a wish but doubt that they will be able to realise it in the near future.

3.2.3 Employees in small family businesses

The employees identify intensely with the business

Two employees answered the question about the work climate with "good", one with "super" and another one with "very good". They could all identify with the business and the work they are doing.

> *(the work climate is – the author)..."good, no problem at all. You grow together, you can't avoid it. Everybody has to do everything."*
> (employee at coMa GmbH)

> *"I can identify with the work. I like the work and I am behind it."*
> (employee at the Götterspeise company)

> *"I identify totally with the business. We know each other privately, too, although we don't do much together outside the business. But the personal side makes it possible for me to take on responsibility for the firm."*
> (employee at Prägo-Patrizen)

In all cases the interviewed employees also have a personal relationship with the boss. It is this involvement by friendships that promotes a "total identification with the business" as one employee at Prägo-Patrizen calls it. A working relationship of sometimes long-time-standing has led to a trusting relationship within and outside the company. They meet up privately, goes to a sports club together, goes out together with the kids or sees one another for other leisure activities.

> "I go to a sports club with one of the bosses and he confides in me. We work well together."
> (employee at coMa GmbH)

The relationship among the people is described as good to very good

> "The work climate is good, it has always been relaxed, with a lot of helping each other."
> (employee at Prägo-Patrizen)

Question: How would you describe the relationship among the colleagues?

> "Super. The others think of Herr Killat as a colleague, too and not as if the boss stood in front of you."
> (employee at Killat GmbH)

All employees described the atmosphere in the business and the work with other colleagues as good to very good. The readiness to help one another and the co-operative relationship among the colleagues was specifically emphasised. The fact that the boss is regarded as a colleague or a friend contributes to this relationship.

The family is not understood as a block by the employees in the business and family problems carried into the business do not seem to matter for the employees

Question: Do you think of the family as a block in the business?

"No, not at all. I see them as a family, but I also see them individually. I rather feel part of the family. (...) the boss and the senior boss have agreed upon not to talk about private matters in the firm. For that we get together."
(employee at Prägo-Patrizen)

"Not at all, I know the whole family, you automatically learn some things and there are no problems"
(employee at Götterspeise)

We learned in the interviews with the owners, that family problems and tensions, which have built up in the family are carried into the business now and again. According to their own statements, this does not worry the interviewed employees. The family is not regarded as a block by the employees in the sense that you can't win against them, but rather as a unity with all the personal characteristics of each family member working for the business. The employees feel part of the family themselves - and because of that there are treated like that, too: for instance when Frau Grossarth senior brings home-made cake for all of them.

The employees know how the business is doing

> *"Yes, I know enough about the shop, I do everything apart from the books and the shopping. That gives you an insight in the situation."*
> (employee at Götterspeise)

> *"Yes, of course, I do the bookkeeping for the company."*
> (employee at the Prägo-Patrizen company)

> *"Yes, in a way. We only rarely see a semi-annual balance sheet. Sometimes you hear them moaning downright how bad things are going, especially the payment behaviour of the customers. You can imagine what it's like, you can do calculations, we know each other privately after all. When a situation concerns us we are informed."*
> (employee at coMa GmbH)

On the whole the interviewed employees feel well informed about the economic situation of the business. Everybody said, that there is no "secret policy" on behalf of the owners, even though you "only" know through the moaning about the payment behaviour how the business is doing.

We have to qualify our report insofar as the interviews were held with the rather better informed employees; the total picture would probably be slightly different.

Employees are included in the decisions

All interviewed employees stated that they are informed about happenings and changes in the business. Two employees have a share in the decision-making that concern the business. Another employee could confirm this for the times that she worked more in the business.

> *"I am definitely included. Everything is more or less talked about together. Purchases, changes and so on."*
> (employee at Götterspeise)

> *"I have to differentiate there: When I was still working full time here, without my child, then that was the case, I was included and took part in conversations which led to decisions: ever since I work here only two afternoons this naturally is no longer the case: it was hard for me to let go."*
> (employee at the Prägo-Patrizen company)

Question: Do you still get to know about decisions despite working less?

"Oh, yes, definitely. Either by being directly told about it or I noticed changes myself and ask."
(employee at the Prägo-Patrizen company)

"We are informed, you are asked what you think about such and such and you have a say, too. Whereas I must say, that too much democracy can be bad, when you have to vote on everything and anything. Doesn't work if you discuss yourself to death."
(employee at coMa GmbH)

None of the employees feel passed over or badly informed. All convey the impression that they get to know about the decision-making in the business and are more or less involved, too. For one employee it was, in fact, almost too much participation.

Proposals for improvement and criticism are possible

All employees stated that they can make proposals for improvement all the time. One employee emphasised that she gets the chance to realise improvements herself. Another employee reported that the business does set limits and that it is necessary to take business planning into consideration.

"That is possible and is received positively by the boss. It is regarded as a help and I can bring in my proposals or criticism quite naturally. I am not afraid to do that and don't have to think about it the day before, how I am going to say it."
(employee at the Prägo-Patrizen company)

"I can bring in my proposals and presume that it would be done. There haven't been a lot of examples for it as yet. As for the rest, when I have a better idea, say concerning a certain dish, then I would just change it and tell the others. That is o.k. We talk about the shop privately a lot and there I can make suggestions for improvement."
(employee at Götterspeise)

"In the sense 'I want that to be different', I can't say here I want other working hours or other holidays. It is like it is. There are no ways to change that. If one of us deviates, then everything is out of gear and breaks down somehow. We depend on one another, that is the principle."
(employee at coMa GmbH)

On the whole the impression is confirmed that has already come to light in the interviews with the owners. Criticism and proposals for improvement are desired and are brought in by the employees. This certainly contributes to the co-operation with the bosses being described down the line as good.

> "Our co-operation is good. Nicole tells me what there is to do and that is o.k. Wolfgang rather does what I tell him to do. He has other tasks."
> (employee at Götterspeise)

There is hardly any formalised controlling

The interviewed employees confirm the statements of the owners, that there is hardly any formalised controlling in the businesses under investigation. Where there is an attendance recording, the employees do not feel controlled by it, but see it as a legitimate instrument of the business. The employees share the assessment of the owners in this point, that things don't really work without mutual trust.

> "I don't feel controlled in the slightest. We fill out our time sheets, but that relies on trust. I can write what I like and when I go out and buy something, I can write down what I choose. No, there is no control and I couldn't tell you how that could be done. We write everything down, pay for it and that's it."
> (employee at Götterspeise)

> "We have an attendance recording, I wouldn't call that controlling mechanisms, that is a legitimate instrument."
> (employee at coMa GmbH)

There is usually no time for training programmes, but not a lack of interest

None of the interviewed employees has taken part in any training schemes in the last few years. The employees did, however, emphasise an interest in specific qualifying.

> "No, there haven't been any offers of qualifying schemes for me. I would go, though, if the topic was interesting and it would help me for my future. It is, however, difficult to take part in a training. There are only three of us down here and then one would be missing."
> (employee at coMa GmbH)

> "Not at the moment, we did go for the IT, yes, but should something arise the company would support it."
> (employee at the Prägo-Patrizen company)

> "No, but possible. Qualification, not in the basics, I have those, beyond that I would be interested."
> (employee at Götterspeise)

The management style is not regarded as authoritarian

Question: What is the management style in the company like?

"Relaxed management style. In my last firm you worked against the boss, when you get on well you don't stay at home because of a minor cold. I get on a lot better with a personal management style."
(employee at Killat GmbH)

"Not at all authoritarian. Not hierarchical in the classical sense either, I would say: extended democracy with partly too democratic characteristics. In certain situations it should be clearly stated what's up, by the bosses I mean."
(employee at coMa GmbH)

"Very co-operative, understanding, not enough of the boss for the realisation of certain matters. That's not her thing. On an equal basis always, as a boss she has her problems sometimes."
(employee at the Prägo-Patrizen company)

Whereas all employees describe the management style of the owners as co-operative, relaxed, and in no way authoritarian, two employees state, that such a co-operative management style can also lead to problems e.g. when the boss is too hesitant about making decisions.

The employees would stand in for the boss

As the employees feel involved in decisions, can contribute criticism and proposals for improvements, and the whole business situation is relaxed and co-operative, it is understandable that they are prepared to stand in for the boss in the case of illness.

> *"Yes, that would be possible and I have already done that, when the boss was on holiday for four weeks."*
> (employee at the Prägo-Patrizen company)

> *"I would do that, whether I could do it in all fields is the question. I haven't tried it, but it would be a challenge that I would take up."*
> (employee at coMa GmbH)

> *"Yes, as far as possible. My colleague too. We know the shop quite well. You have to."*
> (employee at Götterspeise)

Special features of small family businesses

Two employees could not think of anything typical to the question about the special features of small family businesses, because they had no means of comparison with other businesses. One employee said, that the understanding among the people is better than in non-family businesses. The fourth employee was not sure, but said that there are rather specific features of small businesses, whether with or without family.

SMALL. FAMILY. BUSINESSES.

> *"The understanding is better. When you have problems in another business, the boss just says that you have to manage on your own."*
> (employee at Killat GmbH)

Two employees regard it as an advantage to work in a small family business. One employee prefers working for a small business, whether with or without family and another employees believes that the decisive factor are the people with whom you work, be it in a small company, a family business or in a large company.

> *"I don't know, if I were working under the same circumstances as now and the company was managed by two colleagues I would work here, too. It is nicer to work in a small business. It functions better and it is more individual. Better stay small."*
> (employee at coMa GmbH)

> *"Yes, I see an advantage. Although the small business is the reason for me, that is even without family. The advantage is the size, clear structures. One person, who says what's on. That is an absolute advantage. The competencies are clear, not like in a larger business. The business is more manageable and misunderstandings aren't possible. The communication is from person to person. There are no competency problems. That's why everything works here. I know quite clearly and definitely what I have to do and who I can ask when I have a problem."*
> (employee at Götterspeise)

"I don't know whether the family structure plays such a role; I think it depends more on the people."

(employee at the Prägo-Patrizen company)

Focus Employees

On the whole a large degree of identification of the interviewed employees with their work in the SFB was noted. The personal relationship to the owners that you can call trusting and friendly in character contribute to that as well as the general good work climate. The family is not seen as a block in the business and family problems carried into the business do not seem to worry the employees. The interviewed employees all feel informed about the situation of the business, they have an influence on the processes in the business, can voice criticism, and bring in proposals for improvements. For this they put up with the fact there are no training schemes and little flexible holiday arrangements. Because they are involved in the development of the business, they are open and dedicated: They are all prepared to stand in for their boss in emergencies.

The clear structures are regarded as an advantage and are sometimes missed, when the management style is "co-operative"

> It is remarkable that only one employee can name special features of SFBes. Special features are seen more in comparison between small companies and large companies, whereas the fact that a family runs the business does not seem to play a big role for most of the employees.

3.2.4 Résumé: Special Features, Advantages and Disadvantages of small Family Businesses

Self-assessment and observation

> "It is nice to have the family together in the business. The precondition is a sound partnership, that you come together and talk about personal matters, or I take my wife with me when I have an appointment in Cologne and we go out afterwards: such things can be done sometimes."
> (Herr Mörsheim, Mörsheim-Allergieservice)

> „It has advantages to be a family business. Work and looking after the children are easy to organise for us."
> (Herr Golz, Götterspeise)

"There are some positive sides, I have seen the children grow up. What man can say that. I was always at home. You can combine personal and professional matters well at home."
(Herr Mörsheim, Mörsheim-Allergieservice)

"Blood is thicker than water. I would like to have more brothers! The high rate of fluctuation of the employees is a problem; if I had more brothers that wouldn't be a problem! I see the family structure as a huge advantage."
(Andreas Conrad, coMa GmbH)

Six of the eight owners of the interviewed SFBes see advantages for the business and the family through the special business structure. None of the interviewed owners see disadvantages for the business. They did name some disadvantages for the family. Two owners saw neither advantages nor disadvantages.

The brothers Andreas and Frank Conrad of coMa GmbH see a definite advantage in the fact that a large number of family members with their various know-how and abilities work in the business (half of the total of 10 employees belong to the family). It is emphasised that one is on one "line" (Frank Conrad, coMa GmbH) in the family and that the level of trust among family members is totally different to that in non-family businesses. The sometimes very long absences and working hours of the two brothers and the problems resulting from this in the families are named as a disadvantage for the family situation.

Herr Goß of the Elektro Goß company calls it an advantage to have the structure of an SFG, because the customers seek the friendly conversation, which makes for a much greater closeness to the customer, which again could be a market advantage. The advantages for the business are clear here, and the disadvantages lie mainly in having too little time for the family.

The Killat family regards a family business as more customer friendly, as it has a family and personal structure. The family contact with the customer is definitely seen as an advantage over non-family businesses. The customers want this contact. Too little time for the children is seen as a disadvantage for the family.

Even though Herr Mörsheim of the Mörsheim-Allergieservice does not see a particular advantage of his type of business, he does emphasise, that it was a good situation for him to be able to watch his children grow up and see their development. Owing to the work situation in his family business, the work in the business and the work at home were easy to combine with the upbringing of the children.

The family Golz/Hofen of the Götterspeise company sees advantages for the business and the family. Both owners of Götterspeise want the personal contact with their customers. Both want to present their business through their personality and a good service. For the family it is important that the looking after the children is good to organise in the framework of the every day running of the business, and that it is easy to combine with the demands of the business. Both see this as an advantage and are sure that that would not be possible in that way in a 'different' job. Another advantage is seen in being to save costs easier that way.

> "We have less costs altogether than if we had to pay ourselves as employees. We can save on ourselves, that is more difficult with employees."
> (Herr Golz, Götterspeise)

Herr and Frau Rauen of the Baugeschäft Rauen regard it as an advantage to be able to work independently and self-determined. The family sees itself as a unity and everybody performs its contribution to the business. The advantage of an SFB for the customer lies in the close contact to the business. The co-operation is more direct and personal and the customer gets what he wants sooner. Disadvantages are seen in too little time for the family and for changes, which they have in mind for the business.

The self-determined work is, however, in some ways a self-exploitation. You would never put demands to the Employees that you put to yourself.

> "That is because family businesses are often situated in close vicinity to the home and therefore can be exploited more easily. This wouldn't be possible in other firms. This has something to do with self-exploitation. I wouldn't ask an employee to stay in the evening, but when my mother is there..."
> (Frau Grossarth jun. Prägo-Patrizen)

Both the Mayer & Heck and the Prägo-Patrizen company do not see any advantages or disadvantages in being a family business.

Despite sometimes immense hours, which go to the debit of the family life and the intruding of the business in leisure time and private sphere, the owners still see a number of advantages that the business has for the family: the feeling of belonging together, for instance, develops from the joint responsibility and work, and the possibility of a self-determined shaping of one's life also regards the combining of work and family - sometimes even for the men.

It seems to be an advantage for the business to be managed by a family. When two partners (by marriage) have built their life plan on it, they are prepared to invest an immensely large amount of time and work here.

Many customers value this great engagement of family businesses, which they can e.g. reach on the phone at unusual times. The very personal contact between business and customers, which a number of the interviewed businesses emphasised strongly is surely partly due to the family atmosphere giving off to the outside. Many customers value this closeness; some, e.g. older people probably even depend on getting support beyond the pure business side.

Whereas most investigated businesses can fall back on acquaintances and family members in the case of illness, who would then carry on running the business for them, problems can nevertheless arise if "security systems" are not thought about in good time.

4 Résumé and outlook

The aim of the presented study is to name the special preconditions, under which small family businesses work; to determine the specific factors, which facilitate or aggravate their subsistence on changing markets

There are a number of preconditions for their subsistence that the majority of the small family businesses shares with other businesses, e.g.:

like other small companies

- the structure is relatively **lucid** owing to the small size of the business, (that has consequences for the internal communication, work organisation, etc. – also for the personal relationships)
- as a rule people **work a lot**
- **lack of time** is mostly a permanent problem
- **flexibility and diversity** are characteristics demanded of the employees (there are not trained specialists available for every working field; in bottleneck situations everybody has to work everywhere)
- **capital resources** are often rather meagre

Small companies are usually very capable of flexibility owing to their small size: information has a short way to go, that shortens the speed of reaction, and the personal relationship, which arises in very small circles of colleagues, favours the readiness to share the responsibility for the work field of another person and e.g. if necessary to stand in for him. Systematic, foreseeing, and offensive planning often falls victim to the "chronic" lack of time, for which reason small companies often act rather reactive, i.e. changes and developments need a direct impetus from outside (e.g. direct customer request, economic pressure, etc.)[9]

4.1 SPECIAL FEATURES OF SMALL FAMILY BUSINESSES

Aside those factors that characterize small companies, there are a number of special features, which result in the small family businesses from the fact that family members run the business and work in it. The central special feature of small family businesses lies in the fact, that **two social systems** penetrate one another, which are separated in the "normal case" in society: the family and the business.

---

[9] cp. Bundesministerium für Wirtschaft (ed.): Arbeitsheft, Kleine und mittlere Unternehmen. Früherkennung von Chancen und Risiken, Bonn 1998

The working person has its role and task in each system: here probably mother/father and housewife/houseman – there boss, financial expert, customer consultant, etc. when he/she works in a normal employment relationship, these systems will hardly ever meet: in a family business they overlap.

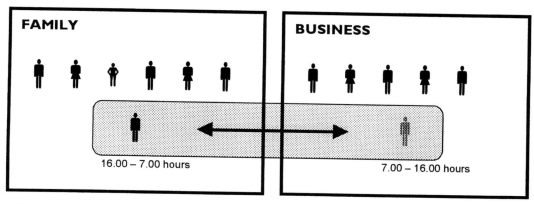

External employment relationship
Family and business are two separate spheres/systems

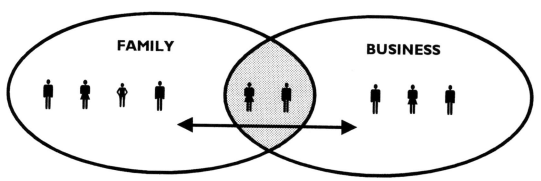

Small family businesses
The systems overlap

Ideally family and business have very differing norms and legal tendencies, in small family businesses these features mix: the family members working together will transfer a part of their family roles, their relationship structure into the business. And the business will with its demands and legal tendencies will effect the family situation in many ways; e.g. it will possibly dictate work and holiday times, influence the mood, maybe even the dealing with one another.

Family	Business
• aim: protecting and maintaining the family • belonging per birth • focus: person	• aim: maximising of profits • belonging per contract • focus: function/performance

In a family business all family members – not only the ones who work in the business – know how the livelihood is earned. Especially when the business premises and the family home are not totally separated the children grow up in the business; different to the children of wage earners, who very often know very little of what is hidden behind the secret "work", where the parents disappear to for many hours per day. At the same time working in your home gives you the chance to watch the children far more than is possible with an external employment: "I have seen the children grow

less alienated work

up" one of our interviewed people emphasised. In fact, a small family business can create possibilities to divide housework and gainful employment flexibly beyond the traditional (sexual) patterns.[10] Many owners, especially those , who come from families with businesses cannot imagine working other than self-employed. As a rule they pay a not insignificant price for being "their own boss". Leisure time and personal relationship are neglected, the same applies to children and the whole family life.

„sometimes I feel sorry for the children..."

Just like the business is always present in the family, so is the fact that the own economic situation depends on the ups and downs of the business; the **dedication** for the business is accordingly high: both for the work and for keeping the other person's back free in peak times. All

---

[10] In principle it would be interesting to take a closer look at the situation of the sexual roles in the families of the small businesses. Compared with the "classical" conservative family situation the work of the women – in family and business - e.g. in traditional crafts families seems to get more recognition , her role is therefore relatively stronger. On the other hand the double burden seems to be especially hard in the business household and it seems as if the work of the women - particularly by the women themselves – is not really seen in its total amount.: The majority of the women interviewed by us underestimated their work load for the business themselves. In this context models for qualifying for these women are of interest. It would also be revealing to have a look at the coverage of such women working in the family business in case of a separation or to take a look at their professional perspectives in case of bankruptcy or closure of the business and if necessary develop concepts for the improvement of their situation.

this contributes to the strong feeling of **belonging** and the depending on one another. And to an accumulation of work (-that the business benefits from-), that very often borders on self-exploitation.

"That has something to do with self-exploitation"

The strong "**we-feeling**" of the family seems to have an effect into the business and cause an atmosphere, which differs from the already very personal closeness in other small companies: because of the family character. In nearly all the businesses interviewed by us we gained the impression that the business itself functions "like a large family"; in fact that even the customers are included in the family "we-feeling". Perhaps this rubbing off of atmosphere is due to the dynamics of the family structure; maybe the owners of family businesses are particularly talented in creating such a trusting familiar situation in the business. Employees feel good in such an atmosphere and work dedicated and motivated. The statement we received on the business situation partly remind of a classical patriarchal family – in the positive sense -; Here the boss is also personally responsible for the well-being of his employees.[11]

Employee:
"I've often felt as if it were my shop"

Boss:
"I have a great responsibility, that person has to feed a family like me."

The customers seem to value this "family atmosphere". The customers have an obvious advantage from this: only a crafts business, where the telephone is in the kitchen at home, can promise permanent direct availability (often even without an answering machine!).

---

[11] The well-meaning "patriarch" also pulls all the strings and, if necessary, limits the insight and influence of his employees: "There are some things that are none of the employees' business"

The family atmosphere also gives them a feeling of trust, belonging and human touch. It is possibly a very specific clientele that this family atmosphere appeals to, which can be used for marketing, if necessary. (accordingly you perhaps find a specific type of employees in small family businesses who fit in these family surroundings?)

Business objectives are family objectives

"...that we always have enough"

Small family businesses therefore have a tendency to include their surroundings in the "we"; employees and customers; "we are all one big family". - on the other hand their core, their motor, and their purpose remains the family. The objective of the business is to feed the family. No less, but primarily no more. The family running a small family business is a "utility unit" (and that means it has an archaic element). Business objectives are inseparably linked with personal family objectives; economic decisions are not directed by the "blind" realisation logic of capital and market, but very centrally by family objectives and requirements. (Example: an important investment for the business is not effected, because the family needs a new sitting-room that year. Or the business fate is only planned around the next few years, because of retirement plans, etc.) so business decisions will often contradict the purely entrepreneurial rules.

4.1 Globalisation as a challenge

As we already mentioned at the beginning (see introduction) 23.5% of all work places in Germany can be found in small companies with less than 10 employees. Europe-wide it is as many as 32%. Most of these small companies are small family businesses. Therefore the relevance of small family businesses from en economic and labour market viewpoint is far greater than for instance that of the coal and steel industry or the motor industry.

We read about the challenges of globalisation to large companies and their handling of it in the papers every day: going public, shareholder value, global player, strategic alliances, lean management, reengineering, Employees reduction, etc. small family businesses are also principally affected by the impact of globalisation: they have to maintain on tighter markets, the competitive pressure is increasing, technologies and products develop and change ever faster, customer demands are growing.

Not all factors of globalisation, however, affect all small family businesses in the same way - at least not at the moment.

Nearly all the small family businesses interviewed by us, stated that their customers have become more demanding, that they expect more in the way of services, consulting, and complete solutions. - those are, however, already all of the common factors of the eight businesses regarding globalisation.

An example for the very differing handling of the new developments are the new **information and communication technologies.** The telephone and the fax machine are standard equipment in all investigated businesses. The necessity for email and presence in the internet is for instance at present regarded as unnecessary, too expensive, too time-consuming by the two classical crafts businesses (interior building, tiles) and also by the Götterspeise company. This might become a problem in the future, as younger customers will rather consult the internet and not the "yellow pages". In contrast the publishing house Mayer & Heck is tackling these two media intensively, as online communication between book shop and publishing houses will probably make the representative superfluous. Other businesses, like the exhibition builders Coma and the electricians Goß are on the way to using this modern means of communication in the future.

"We don't have the time. You have to learn that"

"The customer is going to expect that - I'm sure"

"...with permanent full-employment at present, I don't see an immediate need."

Only a few of the investigated small family businesses have or are developing conceptualised **marketing strategies**. This applies both to the observation of the market and the competitors and to advertising. The personal recommendation, casually called "mouth-to-mouth-propaganda" seems the best - and only - form of advertising to a number of businesses. Those with ample work hardly see the necessity for marketing and advertising. For the tiling business, however, advertisements are a proven means of advertising without which he couldn't "survive". - contrary to the businesses that don't advertise or do so in the traditional way, the allergy service with its a new service has to develop the market actively by observing it intensively Europe-wide and by trying out many different and co-operative information and advertising media also those new to them; and also the exhibition builders whose advertising means are developed in the form of a corporate design.

"…we try different media"

Only one of the interviewed businesses carries out any **controlling** in the closer sense of the word: the exhibition builders CoMa has developed a system of performance controlling over the last few years; this facilitates the preliminary costing and the actual accounting for jobs that take place in far-away places in a business, which is no longer small. The other business owners regard their business as small enough to keep an eye on and their accounting system gives them enough information to be able to do without an economic or performance related controlling system. For this the business culture plays a role: "Controlling" sounds like control, and that creates a bad atmosphere and distrust, which they want to avoid. On the other hand it is a matter of course that the boss controls the completed site.

"If I don't trust a person, then it's no use"

Whether and to what extent small family businesses are affected by the consequences of globalisation and how they react to that depends on factors like:

- **size**
- **competitive situation**
- **market**

the competitive pressure of small family businesses varies a lot. Whereas the electrical business Goß avoids the regional competition by specialising (high-tech lighting), the allergy service Mörsheim and the Prägo-Patrizen company are - at present still? - without competition with their products and services. The Götterspeise company also has no competition in Essen with their biologically oriented lunches.

The latter are oriented on a locally limited market owing to the offered service. This also applies to the two crafts businesses. The other small family businesses, however, have discovered the nation-wide or Europe-wide market. Electrical installations are carried out in Barcelona, stalls are put up at an exhibition in Turin. The allergy service Mörsheim and Prägo-Patrizen also have a Europe-wide or at least transnational perspective with their products and services.

"If I had to work here around the corner, there'd be nothing t gain any more"

Direct triggers play a large role for the businesses' readiness for innovation: the businesses **react** to direct economic pressure and immediate demands of the customers (e.g. the perspective Europe developed for the electrical business, because a Spanish customer approached them). This reactive action is due to a chronic lack of time.

-not least is the personality of the owners the reason for the businesses' dealing with economic change.

For a deeper analysis of the businesses' way of dealing with globalisation the development of a **business typology** would be of interest. - The basic entirety of the businesses investigated in this framework is not sufficient for this, but we can name some categories they could be assigned to like: the classical crafts business with regional orientation (Killat, Rauen), the innovative crafts business with Europe-wide orientation (Goß), small "global players" like the exhibition builders Coma, small monopolistic services (Prägo-Patrizen, Allergieservice Mörsheim), services with little technology with local orientation (Götterspeise), high-tech services with supra-regional orientation (Mayer & Heck).

4.2.1 Support of small family businesses - but how?

In the face of the economic and labour market political importance of small family businesses on the one hand and frighteningly high bankruptcy figures (nearly 90% of all bankruptcies are businesses with up to 20 employees)[12] the question arises: Is there a way to improve the support of these businesses - by

---

[12] verbal statement by the G.I.B. in the framework of the project „Crisis Intervention in Small Companies"; see also G.I.B.-info 2/99, p 28 sqq.

"Only very few call in support"

government institutions, consulting or similar? Of the eight businesses who took part in our investigation, only one had called in support by an organisational consulting and investment help. The others had little or no idea of possible investment, consulting, and other means of support. There was some experience with services from chambers or consulting agencies. These were regarded as too expensive or not practice-related enough. One of the businesses had once bought support from a marketing firm; the owner saw the experience negatively - despite newly gained customers -, because the mailing campaign had been outsized.

There is an existing opinion that this type of business does not need any form of support and consulting and that they do not want it either. After the motto "only the best survive" the ability for self-organisation of the businesses who succeed on the market, increases which strengthens the competitiveness of our economy. On the other hand you have to ask yourself whether we can afford the presently very large number of closures and bankruptcies of small companies - mostly small family businesses - from an economic and social point of view in the long run. The closure of companies, because of the question of succession not having been tackled in time, and bankruptcies could be avoided with early intervention and support. Of course, not every small family business needs consulting and support. But compared to other forms of companies support measures for development processes do not reach these firms often enough - especially seen against their economic importance. From our point of view it would therefore be sensible to adapt consulting and support programmes even better to their demands and to facilitate the availability in order to initiate innovation processes in good time to avoid insolvency[13] etc.

We see a need for action on two levels:

1. the knowledge of the situation, the special features of the small family businesses, etc. has to be increased (research of practice)
2. concepts and instruments of consulting and support must be adapted to the special situation and the particular preconditions of small family businesses.

Need for action

Practice research

The field of the small family businesses has been worked on very little scientifically. A qualitative-oriented action and practice investigation in close connection with small family businesses, pragmatically oriented on the information demand realisable in practice, could close these gaps in one's knowledge. Proceeding from our experience and results following topics, for instance, present themselves:

---

[13] To this the G.I.B has developed approaches in the project mentioned in footnote 12; see also G.I.B.-info 3/99, p 6 sqq.

1. development of a **typology** of small family businesses (see page ?) in order to deduct requirement profiles for innovation processes (globalisation).
2. investigation of the **interplay of business and family system** e.g. with a systematic approach in order to assess chances and risks of such a combination for the business
3. investigation of the **customer groups** of small family businesses (are there customers who have a special affinity to these businesses? Which and why?) in order to be able to maximise the use of specific market advantages
4. investigation of small family businesses founded by **foreign citizens** for a better understanding of their special situation and preconditions
5. investigation of the situation and role of **women in small family businesses** with a view to both their qualifying and influence in the business and their coverage and professional perspective in the case of bankruptcy or separation.

Consequences for consulting and support

The objective of our reflections is to facilitate the approach to specific consulting or other forms of support for those small family businesses whose subsistence could possibly be secured long-term that way.

Now, this is easier said than done. Supporting and consulting businesses whose owners hardly have any time, who usually possess little financial resources and whose competency for diagnosis (what does my business need? Is the regression of turnover a result of a lack of customer orientation, moderate quality or not enough acquisition?) is not sufficiently developed owing to lack of experience or the typical "routine-blindness" to be also found in other forms of companies, is equal to the "squaring of the circle". When a lasting effect of the business development is aimed at, time has to be invested, too, of course. Tailor-made solutions - which are needed, as each family business is different from the next - also cost money, of course. Both is usually more than limited in most small family companies. Despite this difficult starting points we see points of departure for the development of support and consulting approaches.

- **Access to information**

Small family businesses **often don't know anything** about the external help available free of charge, or inexpensive, or at "market prices". These can be development programmes, investment aids consulting promotion, free consulting by the chambers, or other public institutions. The impact of information sent by post is very low accord to our experience. The readiness to think about information increases as a rule when the information is passed on via a personal

personal contacts   contact. For this it is up to tax consultant offices, banks (in their function as creditor) and others to act and look beyond their usual performances and see in their contact with their customer the small family business as an entirety and to look after it. This could also help overcoming another hindrance: It does not correspond with the **family culture** especially in families with a tradition of self-employment to accept help. You have to manage on your own, this claim has a high rating in these families. This is a motor for their great readiness for performance, can also prevent an openness for support from outside. This is a different tendency to the one in business starters or new companies.

internet   Another possibility lies in presenting well-prepared information in differentiated form in the internet with a view to the changed reception habits of the new generation. This also has the advantage that the user can determine time, intensity and duration of getting the information him-/herself.

- **Diagnosis**

As far as we know there are a lot of test procedures, check lists, so-called quick scans, etc. printed or as IT documents – for the diagnosis of the situation of the business, of success and failure factors, the competitiveness, etc., also for small (family) businesses. But these instruments usually do not reach the small family businesses. With one exception: banks use economic instruments of analysis, mainly to establish the risks of their financial commitments and to reduce them respectively. "Red figures" are in many cases only an expression of totally different problems (antiquated products, lack of innovation, lack of or wrong marketing, etc.). As a rule no comprehensive economic consulting and support for innovation processes takes place in this context.

instruments don't reach small family businesses

The access to diagnosis instruments could be improved the same way as the access to the information on e.g. public promotion programmes (see above): in the context of personal relationships (tax consultants, chamber- or bank employees) or by the supply of information via the internet.

The improvement of the access to diagnosis instruments does not necessarily lead to applying the right instrument at the right moment and in the correct place. Often instruments have to be adapted to the respective economic situation. Symptoms of economic deficits often have to scrutinized before diagnosis instruments can be used goal-directed. This is especially the case for the so-called "soft" factors (management style, personnel development, co-operation, etc.) of the business management. Here the business owners as a rule need a vis-à-vis who helps them to focus problems, to equalize their own routine-blindness. In this place we also see a task for those people who are in personal contact with the businesses owing to existing business relationships with the businesses.

- **Consulting**

Management consultants usually calculate their services in days' work. For them the development of consulting products is only worthwhile when they can use those several times and bill respectively large days' work contingents. This is opposed to the situation of the small family businesses. Aside the high cost arising the ready-made consulting services are often not sufficient for the respective business. A small family business usually does not need a ten-day marketing consulting. In many cases the **diagnosis competence** of the consultants is needed to begin with. The realisation often entails the linking of specific consulting (IT, marketing, technical innovations) with process-oriented support (implementation of new instruments and procedures, team development, etc.). Furthermore the consultants need **evaluation competence** regards the **interplay of business and family system.** Decisions in small family businesses are not exclusively come to by entrepreneurial principles. At least equally important, sometimes in the foreground, are family related considerations. The interaction and the role distribution of the family members (in many cases a married couple) has to be considered in the consulting and the development of solution scripts.

The specific situation of small family businesses puts high demands on the consulting competency. At the same time the earnings are comparatively low as against to other consulting fields. The development of the EU-promoted **labour market programmes** in North

Rhine-Westphalia is probably a step in the right direction. In the future the consulting and the qualifying of small family businesses will be funded by up to 1.000 DM per days' work. This will enable consultants to develop a reasonable consulting and qualifying service .

A lot of what applies to the consulting of small family businesses also applies to the development of qualifying services for this target group. In this case, too, it is important to develop and provide reasonable, business-related and made-to-measure qualifying possibilities that can be managed flexibly regards time. The possibilities of the internet are very useful for this purpose. There are already qualifying and teaching forms in which the material can be called upon via the internet and the contact to lecturers is effected over long distances online.[14] Such forms of qualifying gives great flexibility in time, the controlling of the learning speed by the participants and they save the time for travelling.

---

[14] Cp. Project HILKO-Minerva-online: Handwerksfrauen im Lern- und Kooperationsverbund der GIP - Gesellschaft für Informationstechnologie und Pädagogik am IMBSE e.V. in Moers

5 Literature

Amt für amtliche Veröffentlichungen der Europäischen Gemeinschaften (ed.):
Daten 1994-1995, Fünfter Bericht, Unternehmen in Europa, Luxemburg 1995

Ballarini, Klaus, Keese, Detlef:
Die Struktur kleiner Familienunternehmen in Baden-Württemberg, Heidelberg 1995

Ballarini, Klaus, Keese, Detlef:
Strukturen in kleinen Familienunternehmen, in: Veröffentlichungen des Instituts für Mittelstandsforschung, Universität Mannheim (ed.): ifm-Infodienst, Nr. 1, 1999

Brun-Hagen Hennerkes (ed.):
Unternehmenshandbuch Familiengesellschaften: Sicherung von Unternehmen, Vermögen und Familie, Köln u.a. 1998

Bundesministerium für Wirtschaft (ed.):
Arbeitsheft, Kleine und mittlere Unternehmen. Früherkennung von Chancen und Risiken, Bonn 1998

Dahle, Gabriele, Schrader, Michael:
controlling für kleinbetriebe und dienstleister – projektbericht, pragma gmbh Bochum 1998

Keese, Detlef:
Die Bedeutung der mithelfenden Familienangehörigen im Handwerk, in: Fauth-Herkner, Angela (ed.): Der Faktor Humankapital im Handwerk, Duderstadt, 1997, p. 207-235

Leicht, René:
Der Beschäftigungsbeitrag kleinerer Betriebe in längerfristiger Sicht, in: Ridinger, R. (ed.), Gesamtwirtschaftliche Funktionen des Mittelstandes, Berlin 1997

Leicht, René, Stockmann, Reinhard:
Entwicklungsmuster kleinbetrieblicher Prosperität, in: Veröffentlichungen des Instituts für Mittelstandsforschung, Universität Mannheim (ed.): Grüne Reihe, Nr. 8, 1991

Nationale Unterstützungsstelle ADAPT der Bundsanstalt für Arbeit (ed.):
ADAPT-News Nr. 24, Bonn 1999

Simon, Fritz, B.:
Familien, Unternehmen und Familienunternehmen, in: Organisationsentwicklung, 18. Jahrgang, Basel, 1999, Nr. 4, S.16-23

Universität Witten/Herdecke (Hrsg.):
Nachschrift zum II Kongress für Familienunternehmer 6./7. November 1998, Witten 1999

Wimmer, Rudolf, u.a.:
Familienunternehmen – Auslaufmodell oder Erfolgstyp?, Wiesbaden 1996

Ballarini, Klaus, Keese, Detlef:
Entscheidungen im Lebenszyklus kleiner Familienunternehmen, in: Internationales Gewerbearchiv, Heft 1, 1992

Berger, Johannes:
Kleinbetriebe im wirtschaftlichen Wandel, Frankfurt u.a. 1990

Katzendobler, Eva-Maria:
Führung in gewachsenen Organisationen: Chancen und Herausforderungen für wachsende Familienbetriebe im Handwerk, Universität München, Diss., 1998

Leicht, René, Strohmeyer, Robert:
Beschäftigungsbeitrag und Wachstumsmuster kleiner Betriebe, in: Faltin, G., Ripsas, S., Zimmer, J., (ed.): Entrepreneurship. Wie aus Ideen Unternehmer werden, München 1998

Leicht, René, Tur Castello, Joana:
Qualifikation in Kleinbetrieben, Strukturen und längerfristige Entwicklungsmuster in Westdeutschland, in: Veröffentlichungen des Instituts für Mittelstandsforschung, Universität Mannheim (ed.): Grüne Reihe, Nr. 33, 1998

Wassermann, Wolfram:
Kleinbetriebe in Europa: Materialien zu Fragen ihrer „Europatauglichkeit", zu Perspektiven der Firmenkooperation und zur Rolle der Gewerkschaften im KMU-Bereich, Hans-Böckler-Stiftung, Düsseldorf 1994

Westerholt, Birgit:
Die Unternehmer-Ehefrau als Führungskraft. Ein Leitfaden, Wien 1998